HOME AND WORKSHOP GUIDE TO SHARPENING

HOME and WORKSHOP GUIDE to SHARPENING

By HARRY WALTON

POPULAR SCIENCE

HARPER & ROW
New York, Evanston, San Francisco, London

Library of Congress Catalog Card Number: 67-10840
ISBN: 0-06-014523-4
First edition, 1967
Eight Printings

Second Edition, Revised and Updated, 1976
Fifth Printing, 1978

Manufactured in the United States of America

CONTENTS

CHAPTER ONE

ANATOMY OF A CUTTING EDGE

Even a brand-new tool of good make isn't necessarily at its sharpest, though many a buyer will assume it is and be content with it. This is unfortunate, for it cheats him of the fun of using a keen tool.

Some time ago I tested a new $200 high-speed circular saw. Its gleaming 10″ chrome-alloy blade looked highly competent. To my surprise, it took much more feed pressure than I expected to push a four-by-four into it, and when it finally did cut through, both the cut surfaces were very rough.

Unconvinced that a new blade could be at fault, I removed it and substituted one from my older saw, an old blade I had myself resharpened some weeks before. It sliced through the same stock in less time and with much less pressure—and both the cut surfaces were smooth. Later I told a sales officer of the company that makes the machine (but not the blade) about this. "I'm not surprised," he answered. "First thing our salesmen do when they take out a new demonstrator is remove the blade and have it sharpened."

This doesn't mean that all new tools are dull when you buy them. Many are in top shape. Probably the manufacture of the saw blade in question has been modified for the better since my experience. But tool makers' policies and practices do vary. Also, a rushed worker or a tired inspector may let an imperfectly sharpened tool slip through. So it pays to be suspicious, not only of new tools that prove disappointing in use, but doubly so of your own tried and trusted ones. Sometimes even these can let you down.

To repair a broken seat bracket in an imported car, I got out an electric drill and a valued set of high-speed twist drills. I use these only occasionally, reserving a cheaper set for most jobs. But this time the drill selected failed miserably. I did everything but stand on it; the drill would make no more than a dimple, and I wondered what super alloys the French used for seat brackets. In desperation I finally looked at the drill through a magnifying glass. It was as dull as a treasurer's report. After sharpening, it waltzed right through that same car bracket with no hesitation.

This points up two facts. One is that even the best and sharpest of tools will become dull if it is used often enough. The other is that a tool driven by power (an electric drill in this case) may become duller and duller without our realizing it, because the motor, rather than your muscles, supplies the extra effort to push dull edges through.

If you have never used really keen tools, you may not know what you're missing. The sawing that is sheer drudgery, the chisel work that looks as if beavers did the job, the bored holes that leave you sweating or the bit smoking, are probably caused by dull edges. Sharp saws, keen chisels, well-sharpened bits are more fun to use, besides doing better work. The same holds true for household and garden tools, from scissors to spades.

Strangely, too, sharp tools are actually safer than dull ones. The latter can cut you just as badly, and are more likely to, because a dull tool often has to be forced and is more prone to slip. Sharp tools are more economical. They save you time, effort, and money. Once an edge is dull, it's on the ·road to worsening. Timely resharpening not only restores the edge's cutting ability, but makes it last longer.

Many tool users shun trying to do their own sharpening, possibly because of a failure or two. This isn't unusual, for sharpening is a curiously subtle operation. The less metal you remove to achieve your end, the better. But where you remove it, and what shape you leave the edge in, are all-important factors. If you think that makes sharpening a precision job, you're quite right. But this doesn't mean it's beyond anyone who will take the time and trouble to learn a few basic facts.

THE SHAPE OF THINGS THAT CUT. Just what is it that enables one material to cleave another? Relative hardness is one important characteristic, of course. A wooden paddle can slice butter, cast iron can scratch brass, and hardened steel will cut unhardened steel. But even the hardest material won't cut another unless it is given a certain crucial shape—namely an edge.

The entering edge that starts a cut should be as thin as practicable. In razors its width would be measured in hundred-thousandths of an inch. But a razor won't stand up to cutting wood; it will break down because it is too brittle, and also because there isn't enough metal immediately behind the edge to back it up. To put it another way, its edge bevel is too acute.

This edge bevel is the angle between the two sides that meet to form the edge (Figure 1). It makes most cutting tools a special kind of wedge, capa-

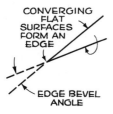

CONVERGING
FLAT
SURFACES
FORM AN
EDGE

EDGE BEVEL
ANGLE

Fig. 1. Edge bevel angle is formed by sides of cutting tool meeting to form a wedge.

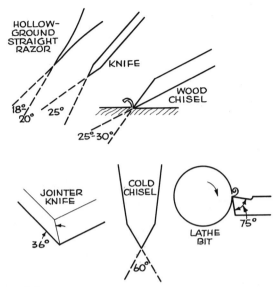

Fig. 2. Cutting tools have different bevel angles according to the purpose for which they are used.

ble of getting "under the skin" to split off a slice, a chip, or a shaving. But the wedge must be hair-thin on a razor, thicker on a carving knife, still heavier on a jointer blade, and downright chunky on a cold chisel (Figure 2). On some machining bits, the bevel angle becomes even more obtuse. For cabinet scrapers, which produce extremely smooth wood surfaces, it is a full 90 degrees.

The strength required back of the cutting edge to make it withstand the shock of the work also determines the blade bevel, or the shape of the blade above the edge bevel (Figure 3). It may be the slim taper of a razor, or the blunt wedge of an axe. On razors, knives, and many other tools the blade bevel is not touched in sharpening. But some tools, including plane irons and wood chisels, may wear so far back as to require reshaping of the blade bevel.

SAW TEETH YOU CAN'T SEE. Under the microscope, even the keenest razor looks like a Stone Age saw. Instead of a straight line, it presents a row of ragged notches. But put a dull blade under the lens, and you'll see a difference. The notches are bigger—both wider and deeper (Figure 4).

The metal at the base of a notch is obviously thicker than at its ends, as the drawing shows. It is no longer an edge there; the blade has lost that much of its cutting ability. It must tear rather than cut, and the surface it

Fig. 3. Blade bevel angle is determined by the strength required back of a cutting edge.

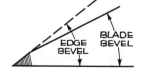

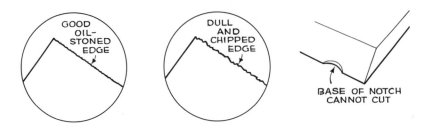

Fig. 4. Microscopic view of a keen edge looks slightly ragged, but a dull edge shows deep notches which tear instead of cutting.

leaves will be correspondingly rough. Worse still, dullness becomes aggravated with use. Each of the noncutting notches becomes a stress point. The shock of being advanced into material they cannot cut tends to enlarge the notches, breaking down the edge still farther.

Proper sharpening reduces the raggedness of the edge contour and can give us not merely serviceable, but even superb tools. A well-sharpened plane iron has been known to peel off a single wood chip 10 feet long. Maine woodsmen who take pride in keeping their axes sharp have been known to shave with them. You needn't go that far, but you will enjoy using tools that are truly sharp.

Boring tools. These facts about cutting edges apply to those on twist drills and auger bits too. Though rotary tools, these have perfectly straight cutting edges. A cross section of a twist drill would show that the edge bevel is fairly obtuse, as it must be to cut metal. In an auger bit it is more acute, a difference equally evident between a metal-cutting cold chisel and a wood chisel.

On handsaws and circular saws, the crosscut teeth that sever wood fibers have their edges at the front (Figure 5). Ripsaw teeth, and the raker teeth of combination circular saws, are different. They lift out shavings like miniature chisels, and indeed resemble chisels, having their teeth at the very tip, straight across the blade.

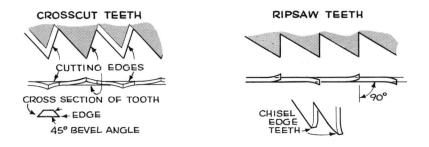

Fig. 5. Comparison between crosscut-saw teeth and ripsaw teeth. Crosscut-saw teeth have the cutting edges at the front; ripsaw teeth at the tip.

HOW SHARPENING WORKS. The cure for the dull condition shown in Figure 4 is to remove metal back to the bottom of the deepest notch. If undertaken in time, this can be done by whetting the edge bevel only. It is important to maintain the correct bevel angle for the tool. Obviously, too, the less metal removed in the process, the longer the tool will last.

Remember that the notches in question are microscopically small, though their relative magnitude is important. Any nicks big enough to see with the naked eye are gross defects that must be remedied before proper sharpening can be done. A nicked blade must be ground back far enough to remove the nicks, which may involve reshaping the blade bevel. With modern grinding wheels, this is no great chore.

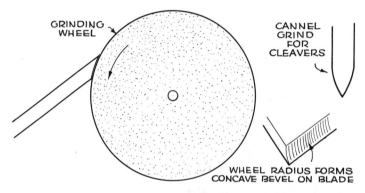

Fig. 6. Hollow-ground edges are sharpened on the periphery of a grinding wheel, producing a concave bevel. Heavy-duty edges for meat cleavers are ground with a convex bevel, or cannel grind.

When you bring home a new edged tool of any kind, it is a good idea to examine it closely and even to measure the bevel angles. Circular saws especially are so complex that you may want to jot down the information, and make an outline tracing of the original tooth shape, against the day a new blade needs resharpening.

What hollow grinding means. An edge is formed where the two flat planes of an edge bevel meet. But if the bevel is ground on the periphery of a grinding wheel, instead of on the side or on a bench stone, it will not be flat, but will have a radius equal to that of the wheel (Figure 6). This concavity brings the sides almost parallel at the very edge, producing an edge even sharper than one with a flat-ground bevel. Because there is less metal directly behind the edge, however, it is also somewhat weaker.

A hollow-ground blade bevel on wood chisels and plane irons makes it easier to distinguish the edge bevel during final whetting. On scissors and razors the entire blade bevel is usually hollow ground. But where the edge must stand up to hard shocks, as on wood-turning chisels, a flat bevel is preferable to a hollow-ground one. Heavy-duty edges like those on meat cleavers, on the other hand, are ground with a convex bevel, called a cannel grind, the direct opposite of a hollow-ground one (Figure 6).

A feather edge, or wire edge, is a phenomenon that occurs during sharpening. As metal is removed, the extreme edge becomes so thin that it bends back (Figure 7). Readily felt with the fingers, this wire edge is a sign that the edge has been whetted sufficiently, but it is itself too weak to be of use, and dulls the working edge. The wire edge is removed by whetting the opposite face of the blade, or by rubbing across a piece of hardwood, which breaks it off. Final light honing then leaves a keen, serviceable edge on the blade.

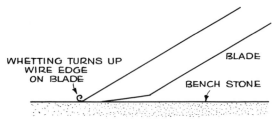

Fig. 7. Wire edge turns up on top of blade during whetting, indicates blade is sufficiently sharp. It is removed by whetting the opposite face of the blade.

Where metal is removed for sharpening is very important. The right place depends largely on what kind of tool it is, and in part on how dull the edge has become.

In theory, the edge shown at A in Figure 8 could be sharpened by grinding back either of the bevels far enough to remove the rounding of the edge. But the two methods at B and C can be ruled out. Though they would leave a sharp edge, it would have a different edge bevel than the original. Assuming that the one put on by the tool maker is best for that particular tool, such a drastic change is undesirable.

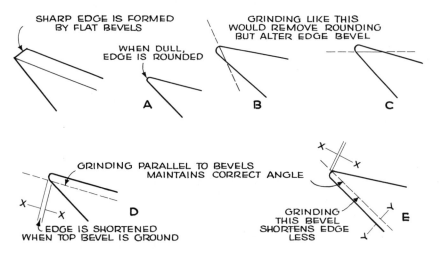

Fig. 8. Removing metal from the right place when sharpening a rounded edge in order to maintain the correct edge bevel for the particular tool.

The rounding can be removed by grinding the upper bevel as at D, so preserving the original angle. (Light whetting or honing on the opposite bevel to remove the wire edge may be ignored for the moment.) This will bring back the edge, or in effect shorten the blade, by the amount x-x in the drawing. Should shortening in this direction be undesirable, we can instead remove metal from the other bevel as at E. The x-x shortening is much less, the edge being brought back in the direction y-y instead.

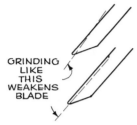

GRINDING
LIKE
THIS
WEAKENS
BLADE

Fig. 9. Wrong way to sharpen a plane iron or a wood chisel.

What this means in practice is shown in the other drawings. Trying to sharpen a wood chisel or a plane iron by grinding the flat side of the blade as in Figure 9 would leave either a long taper or a step in it, both weakening the blade greatly. Obviously the short bevel should be ground. Certain circular-saw blades (Figure 10) can better be sharpened by grinding or filing the tops of the teeth rather than their fronts. Top sharpening is easier, saves time, and does not affect the angle of the front or face grind.

Fig. 10. Sharpening circular-saw teeth on the top does not affect the angle of the front or face grind.

SAW TEETH
MAY BE FILED
OR GROUND
ON TOP

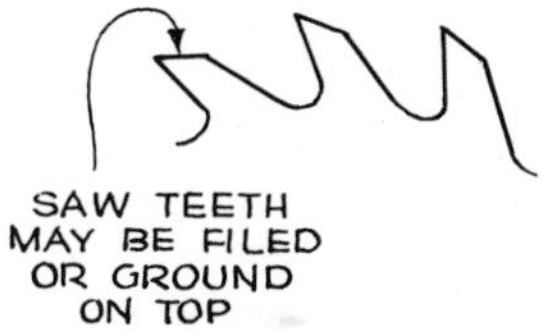

Top sharpening will, of course, shorten the teeth radially, making the saw blade slightly smaller in diameter. This doesn't matter in a circular saw (except that it slightly reduces its maximum depth of cut). It is only necessary to make certain all the teeth are shortened equally.

But screw taps or machine reamers are a different matter. Grinding the tops of the reamer teeth in Figure 11 would shorten them and so change the diameter of the reamed hole, impairing the tool's integrity. Therefore a tap or a reamer is stoned only on the fronts of the teeth, inside its flutes. Unless wear has been excessive, this will not affect the working diameter enough to matter, as already shown at E in Figure 8.

Excessive wear may require reshaping of the blade or the teeth of a tool, and this may involve grinding of both edge bevels. But for ordinary sharpening, a little metal removed from the right place can do wonders.

REAMER TEETH MUST BE
HONED IN FLUTES ONLY

Fig. 11. Grinding tops of reamer teeth would shorten them, changing the diameter of the reamed hole.

CHAPTER TWO

WHAT YOU CAN USE FOR SHARPENING

THE same edge can be sharpened on a grinding wheel, on a sheet of abrasive paper, or with a handstone. Skill and judgment, which anyone can develop with practice, count for more than equipment. Though this chapter will cover almost every kind of sharpening equipment available for home and amateur workshop use, don't be led to think you need a great deal of it. Like tools, sharpening materials are best bought as the need for them arises. You'll buy more intelligently and more enjoyably that way, than if you set out to accumulate all the items mentioned at one time.

You may also find that you can make good use of things already on hand. That junked washing-machine motor, for instance, might be converted into a useful grinding head. And some excellent—and speedy—sharpening can be done on the belt sander you thought you bought only for working wood.

FILES CAN SHARPEN a number of edged tools that are not extremely hard. Among these are axes and hatchets, hoes, shovels, spades, lawnmower blades, wood chisels, hedge clippers, auger bits, and spade bits. Files are fairly cheap, and you can take one along to almost any job where an edge may need touching up.

Three or four files—which you'll probably use for other purposes too—may be all you need. A 10″ mill bastard file will be useful for sharpening garden tools such as hoes and spades. For harder blades, finer edges, and shearing tools a second cut mill file or the even finer-toothed smooth mill file can be used.

Handsaw teeth will call for triangular files, called taper files. These come in a sturdy regular taper, and in three other types that taper less but are slenderer—slim, extra slim, and double extra slim. Fine-toothed handsaws with up to 14 teeth per inch are best sharpened with a 5″ double extra-slim file; a 6″ slim taper will serve for sharpening saws with up to 10 points per inch. An accompanying table shows the sizes recommended for saw filing by file manufacturers.

Taper files are for all kinds of saw teeth with a 60-degree angle between them. For sharpening teeth with a lesser angle, there is the cantsaw file, whose sides are at 30 degrees.

Special files for the gardening enthusiast include one of lozenge or diamond section for sharpening pruning saws (it has teeth on two faces of one side, the other two faces being smooth), and a handy 10″ flat file for sharpening rotary-mower blades.

FILE SIZES FOR SAW SHARPENING

Saw points per inch	File
5 to 5½	7″ Regular Taper
6	7″ or 8″ Slim Taper
7 to 8	6″ Slim Taper
9 to 10	5″ or 6″ Slim Taper
11 to 12	4½″ Slim Taper or 7″ Double Extra Slim Taper
13 to 15	4½″ Slim Taper or 5″ Double Extra Slim Taper

FACTS ABOUT ABRASIVES. Whetstones, grinding wheels, sandpaper, and valve grinding compound all abrade metal by the cutting action of thousands of tiny edged particles. These are grains of very hard natural or synthetic substances. Emery, one of the oldest of the natural abrasives, is a granular variety of corundum, a mineral related to the ruby and sapphire. Garnet, once widely used to make a superior sandpaper, is a glasslike mineral akin to the jewel of the same name. Certain quartz deposits in Arkansas, and Ohio blue sandstone, are useful natural abrasives.

But man-made materials now surpass natural abrasives in important respects, being more uniform, and harder than anything found in nature except the diamond. (Diamond dust is an important industrial abrasive.) The synthetic abrasives, made in the electric furnace, are marketed under various trade names. Best known perhaps are those of the Norton Company, pioneers in the field. Norton-made aluminum oxide is known by the trade name of Alundum. The same maker's silicon-carbide abrasive is called Crystolon. A third and even harder product, boron carbide, is used in grain form and molded into such things as blast-nozzle liners and wheel-dresser sticks, but is not suitable for making into whetstones or grinding wheels.

Although natural stones may be merely cut to the desired shape and size, synthetic abrasive is ground and then graded as to the size of grain. This screening is important because if different grain sizes are used together, the larger will do most of the work, besides leaving scratches too deep for the smaller grains to remove.

The grain size, or grit, is designated by numbers ranging from 8 to 600.

These figures refer to the number of holes per linear inch in the finest screen the grains will pass through. It is worth noting that the same grit may be considered fine for one use, coarse for another. Thus No. 80 grit makes a fine-grained grinding wheel but a coarse abrasive paper. Aluminum-oxide paper for finish sanding is 200 or 220 grit, while silicon-carbide paper for hand-finishing plastic prior to buffing should be 400 or 600 grit.

Each grain has several sharp points or edges, and when the abrasive is used in powder form (for valve grinding or machine lapping, for instance) these come into play in random succession. But for most uses the abrasive particles are bound together or to a backing, and only the outermost points are effective. To insure making the most of them, some abrasive papers are electrically charged during manufacture. Electrostatic repulsion between the charged paper and similarly charged particles makes each grain stand on end, literally putting its best point forward.

HAND AND BENCH STONES are the cheapest abrasive sharpening tools you can buy. In good hands they can produce the keenest of edges. The best natural stones are dense, hard, and relatively costly. These are Hard Arkansas stones, quarried from quartz deposits in the Ozark Mountains and used by surgeons, dentists, engravers, ivory carvers, and other craftsmen who require the finest edges. Soft Arkansas stones, at roughly half the cost, are somewhat more porous, softer, and quicker working. Though they won't produce quite as fine an edge as Hard Arkansas stones, they are fully adequate for sharpening most shop tools. A still cheaper natural stone, Queer Creek, is cut from Ohio blue sandstone.

Norton Company's Grinding Wheel Division offers in addition to these natural stones a line of aluminum-oxide stones under the trade name India, and another of silicon-carbide stones under the trade name Crystolon. These synthetic stones are of course not cut like natural ones, but made by bonding together grains of the synthetic materials. India stones, brown in color, produce the keenest edges. The gray Crystolon stones cut faster and are recommended where speed of sharpening is of greater importance than the fineness of the edge. (Hard or Soft Arkansas stones are often used for final honing after sharpening with synthetic stones. This saves wear on the costlier stones while producing edges superior to those that could be obtained on synthetic stones alone.)

Most India and Crystolon stones are oil filled at the factory and so come ready for use, besides soaking up less oil during use. Other stones must be soaked in oil before they are put into service.

A 1″ by 2″ by 8″ India two-grit bench stone costing about $6 is a good choice for sharpening things as diverse as plane irons, scissors, and hunting knives. This high-quality synthetic stone resists wear and grooving, which can soon put a softer stone out of business. For fine work such as touching up a dull countersink, smoothing gear teeth, or dressing a tool bit right in the lathe, the same India abrasive comes in the form of a triangular stick.

In stick form, the abrasive stones are called files. Triangular and square

Two-grit India bench stone is basic sharpening equipment for knives, scissors, plane irons, and similar small cutting tools.

Abrasive sticks for fine work: triangular stick for sharpening countersinks (left); special rectangular stick for auger bits (right).

Slipstones have flat surfaces for sharpening straight-edged tools, rounded edges for concave tools such as gouges and molding knives.

forms come in Hard Arkansas stone as well as synthetic materials. Besides these shapes, there are round, tapering round, oval, diamond, and flat rectangular sections, some designated for specific uses such as sharpening taps and reamers, jointer knives, auger bits, and carving tools. Curved stones are useful for whetting gouges and other curved edges. Crystolon slips will touch up super-hard carbide-tipped lathe bits and saw teeth.

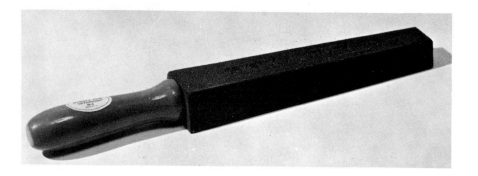

Crystolon wooden-handled stones are available for sharpening everything from knives to garden tools.

Slips or slipstones have a wedgelike cross section, the edges being rounded and one somewhat thicker than the other. The flat surfaces will sharpen straight edges of all kinds. The rounded edges are useful for sharpening concave edges such as those of gouges and molding knives.

For more common chores there are steel-cored knife sharpeners that resist breaking, all-purpose sharpeners consisting of a combination stone (coarse on one side, fine on the other) on a wooden handle, and inexpensive scythestones just right for restoring the edges of scythes, sickles, and brush hooks. The gardener can also make good use of a tapering square-sectioned coarse Crystolon stone fitted to a handle. Called a utility file, it is said to outlast and outperform metal files for sharpening coarse-edged garden implements.

A Crystolon axe stone, in the form of a disk with a rounded edge, has coarse grit on one side and fine on the other. Much cheaper is the same man-

Crystolon combination axe stone has course grit on one side, smooth grit on the other.

Crystolon abrasive stick with grooved sides keeps fish hooks sharp.

ufacturer's single-grit rectangular Queer Creek axe stone, made of Ohio blue sandstone. There are also various small sportsmen's and pocket stones, including a square Crystolon stick with grooved sides for sharpening fish hooks and their barbs.

HOW TO CARE FOR STONES. The first thing to do with a new stone, unless it is one that has been oil-filled at the factory, is to soak it overnight in oil. Probably the best oil for this purpose, and for lubricating the stone when using it, is Bear oil, a Norton Company product. This highly refined mineral oil has the least tendency to "load" the stone by trapping metal and abrasive particles in it.

Next best are medicinal mineral oil, Singer sewing machine oil, Three-in-One oil, and kerosene. An old refrigerator ice-cube tray makes a good tank for soaking stones.

All stones, and that includes oil-filled ones, should be used with a lubricant, preferably Bear oil. Lacking that, use mineral oil or one of the other substitutes, or as a last resort plain water. The lubricating fluid performs an important function. It floats off metal and abrasive dust that would otherwise become embedded in the stone, impeding its cutting action and eventually glazing it to the point of uselessness. Therefore apply oil, kerosene, or water to a stone whenever sharpening anything on it. The oil used for soaking new stones can be used for this purpose. A labeled oil can makes a convenient container and applicator. (Since soaking oil may have some stone particles in it, it should not be used for lubricating anything else.) After each use, wipe the old oil off and apply a little fresh oil before putting the stone away.

Bench stones are best kept in a wooden box with a cover on it, for dust, sawdust, and dirt will load the stone much as sharpening dust will. With the cover removed, the box holds the stone in place for sharpening. Figure 1 shows how to make such a box.

Clean stones occasionally with a stiff fiber brush and kerosene. Resoak in Bear oil or mineral oil after cleaning, and your stones will last for years. If a stone is so badly glazed that brushing with gasoline or lighter fluid doesn't clean it, rub the surface on coarse abrasive paper tacked on a flat surface, then re-oil it.

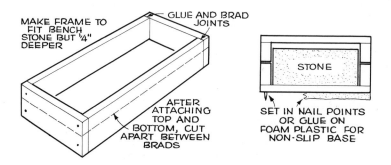

Fig. 1. Wooden box can be made for holding a bench stone in place while sharpening a tool, as well as for keeping the stone clean when not in use.

Careful use will preserve the flat surfaces of even the softer stones. Use the whole surface as much as possible, not merely the center. Turn a bench stone end for end occasionally to equalize wear. For sharpening pointed tools that might gouge the surface, use the side of the stone instead.

OTHER HAND-SHARPENING HELPS. A fair emergency substitute for a bench stone is a wooden paddle faced with abrasive cloth or paper (Figure 2). A coarse grit may be fastened to one side, and a fine grit to the other. The abrasive sheets must be taut and flat for good results. If held on with rubber cement or tacks, they may be stripped off when worn and new sheets applied.

A knife steel such as chefs use for sharpening knives between grindings is a long tapering steel rod fitted to a handle. The rod has very fine grooves along it, and works not by grinding, but by turning up and breaking off a very fine feather edge, so generating a new cutting edge. This can be done

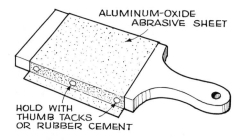

Fig. 2. Wooden paddle faced with abrasive sheet can substitute for a bench stone.

six to eight times before regrinding is called for. Because of the way a knife steel is used, the knife being stroked toward the handle, it should have a guard there to protect the fingers.

The barber's familiar leather strop works much the same way. A similar piece of heavy leather, fastened hair side up to a board or bench and oiled, may be used for honing knives, chisels, plane irons and other fine-edged woodworking tools. Always strop away from the edge—that is, trail the edge across the leather, never push into it.

The wet grindstone was once a familiar sight in farmyards and black-smith shops. It was a fairly big natural stone, 10" or more in diameter, running at low speed in a trough partly filled with water. Such a stone was cool-grinding and could produce excellent edges. Very large wet grindstones are still used in manufacturing the finest cutlery. They are turned away from the edge instead of against it, and the operator can keep tabs on the sharpening process by watching the feather edge turn up before him.

You can buy a wet grinder, with a 1½" thick, 10" diameter sandstone wheel running in a water trough, for about $20. This includes a wheel guard and tool rest, but you will need a ¼-hp. motor to drive it, plus a belt and pulleys to give it a speed of about 125 r.p.m. Nothing surpasses the wet grinder for put-ting a fine edge on cutlery, carving tools, or even a hatchet, but you'd soon wear it out grinding lathe bits to shape or taking deep nicks out of an axe edge. Also, it works slowly and the soft natural stone can readily wear out of round. Take care, if you use a wet stone like this, to drain the water when you're through grinding. If the trough is left filled, that part of the stone left standing in the water can absorb enough to put the wheel badly out of balance.

Today the high-speed grinder is much more common than the wet grind-stone. Except in industrial use, grinding wheels are usually run dry. The work is kept cool by dipping it in water frequently during grinding, or by letting it cool in the air between grinding applications. Unless one constantly keeps the need for cooling in mind, it is easy to "burn" tool edges. This means getting them so hot from grinding friction that the steel turns dark blue, a sure sign that the temper has been drawn not only at the blued edge, but for some dis-tance back.

FACTS ABOUT GRINDING WHEELS. Almost all modern wheels are syn-thetic, made by bonding abrasive grains together in the desired size and shape. There is a vital relation between the grains and the strength of bonding between them. To perform well, a grinding wheel must continuously break down at the working surface. As the sharp points of the abrasive grains are dulled, the bond should let these worn grains break away, exposing sharp new ones to carry on the work. If the bond is too strong and holds dull grains fast, friction will increase as grinding action diminishes. Abrasive and metal dust will fill the pores of the wheel until it is glazed—smooth, shiny, and worthless for grinding. A glazed wheel readily overheats and burns the work applied to it.

Section	CUTLERY or TOOL	COARSE STONING (for restoring cutting edge)	MEDIUM STONING (for average cutting edge)	FINE STONING (for fine cutting edge)	FINISH HONING (for keenest edge desired)	SHARPENING STONES (best suited for each cutting edge listed)
HOME CUTLERY	KNIVES, Jack / KNIVES, Pen / KNIVES, Pocket	SPORTSMAN Stone IBP-34, Coarse side	CRYSTOLON Pocket Stone JP-13 or 14	SPORTSMAN Stone IBP-34, Fine side or FASTCUT Pocket Stone KP-13	HARD or SOFT ARKANSAS Pocket Stone AP-12 or SP-13	
HOME CUTLERY	KNIVES, Kitchen / KNIVES, Paring	CRYSTOLON Combination Benchstone JB-6 or 8, Crs. side	—	CRYSTOLON Sharpener 273-A	—	
HOME CUTLERY	KNIVES, Carving	CRYSTOLON Combination Benchstone JB-6 or 8, Crs. side	KANTBREAK or QUICKCUT Sharpener KPT-2 or 4	CRYSTOLON Combination Benchstone JB-6 or 8, Fine side	SOFT ARKANSAS Benchstone SB-6 or 8	
HOME CUTLERY	CLEAVERS, Meat / SHEARS, Household	CRYSTOLON Combination Benchstone JB-6 or 8, Crs. side	—	CRYSTOLON Combination Benchstone JB-6 or 8, Fine side	SOFT ARKANSAS Benchstone SB-6 or 8	
HOME CUTLERY	SCISSORS, Household	CRYSTOLON Combination Benchstone JB-45 or 134, Crs. side	—	CRYSTOLON Combination Benchstone JB-45 or 134, Fine side	SOFT ARKANSAS Benchstone SB-4	
HOME CUTLERY	RAZORS, Straight	BEAR Razor Hone VR-18, Red side, wet	—	BEAR Razor Hone VR-18, Black side wet	Leather Strop	
SPORT EQUIPMENT	KNIVES, Jack / KNIVES, Pocket	SPORTSMAN Stone IBP-34, Crs. side	CRYSTOLON Pocket Stone JP-13 or 14	SPORTSMAN Stone IBP-34, Fine side or FASTCUT Pocket Stone KP-13	HARD or SOFT ARKANSAS Pocket Stone AP-12 or SP-13	
SPORT EQUIPMENT	KNIVES, Fish / KNIVES, Hunting	SPORTSMAN Stone IBP-34, Crs. side	—	SPORTSMAN Stone IBP-34, Fine side	HARD ARKANSAS Benchstone HB-4	
SPORT EQUIPMENT	HOOKS, Fish	—	CRYSTOLON Fisherman's Stone JT-29	—	—	
SPORT EQUIPMENT	SKATES, Ice	Skate sharpening requires special grinding wheel equipment or the services of a skate sharpening shop		INDIA Benchstone FB-14, deburring	INDIA Round File FF-244, honing	

harpening stone for your purpose...

OUTDOOR TOOLS

CUTLERY or TOOL	COARSE STONING (for restoring cutting edge)	MEDIUM STONING (for average cutting edge)	FINE STONING (for fine cutting edge)	FINISH HONING (for keenest edge desired)
SHEARS, Grass / SHEARS, Pruning	CRYSTOLON Round Edge Slip CJS-44	—	CRYSTOLON Round Edge Slip FJS-44	—
CUTTERS, Weed / SHEARS, Hedge	ALL-PURPOSE Sharpener JT-9, Coarse side	—	ALL-PURPOSE Sharpener JT-9, Fine side	—
AXES / HATCHETS / MACHETES	CRYSTOLON Combination Axe Stone JT-3, Crs. side	—	CRYSTOLON Combination Axe Stone JT-3, Fine side	SOFT ARKANSAS Benchstone SB-4
CUTTERS, Sod / HOES, MATTOCKS / SHOVELS, SPADES	UTILITY FILE JD-2	GENERAL PURPOSE Stone JT-911	—	—
SICKLES / SHEARS, Lopping / SCYTHES	ALUNDUM or CRYSTOLON Scythe-stone TD-1 or TJ-2	HOME & GARDEN Sharpener JT-8, Convex side	WESTERN Scythe-stone TN-13	—
HOOKS, Brush, Grass	—	—	—	—

HOMECRAFT TOOLS

CUTLERY or TOOL	COARSE STONING (for restoring cutting edge)	MEDIUM STONING (for average cutting edge)	FINE STONING (for fine cutting edge)	FINISH HONING (for keenest edge desired)
SAWS	INDIA Taper Triangle CF-544	—	INDIA Taper Triangle FF-544	—
KNIVES, Jointer	CRYSTOLON Jointer Stone JE-74	—	INDIA Jointer Stone IE-74	HARD ARKANSAS Flat File HF-823
GOUGES, Wood	—	INDIA Special Gouge Slip FS-76	INDIA Special Gouge Slip FS-76	—
COUNTERSINKS	INDIA Triangular File CF-134	—	INDIA Triangular File FF-134	HARD ARKANSAS Triangular File HF-133
BITS, Auger	INDIA Auger Bit Stone MT-10	INDIA Auger Bit Stone MT-10	INDIA Auger Bit Stone FT-10	—
BLADES, Plane / CHISELS, Wood / DRAWKNIVES / SCRAPERS	INDIA Combination Benchstone IB-6 or 8, Coarse side	—	INDIA Combination Benchstone IB-6 or 8, Fine side	HARD ARKANSAS Benchstone HB-6 or 8

SHARPENING STONES — best suited for each cutting edge listed (shown as stone-shape illustrations for each tool).

If the bond is too weak, on the other hand, grains will be shed before they are dull and the wheel will wear too rapidly. Aside from economy, this can cause a loss of accuracy. In precision grinding, too soft a wheel may shrink so rapidly that it takes progressively less off each tooth of such tools as circular saws and reamers, so failing to maintain their true diameter.

Obviously a compromise is necessary to suit the grit size, the kind of work to be done, wheel speed, and other factors. The strength of bonding is designated as the *grade* of the wheel, and for industrial wheels is expressed by the letters of the alphabet from A (softest) to Z (hardest). For precision grinding, medium-grade wheels from F to N are usually used, while for rough grinding the harder grades (M to Z) are preferred. A vitrified (glasslike) bond is the most common, though resinoid and rubber bonds are used in high-speed cutoff and other special industrial wheels.

The wheel *structure* must space the abrasive grains far enough apart to let grinding dust fly free instead of packing between the grains, which would "load" it rapidly. For each grit size and grade, there is an optimum structure or spacing. You don't have to worry about it when choosing a wheel, for manufacturers have it down to a science.

But you do have to choose the grit size, and this depends largely on the kind of work in prospect. For really rough grinding like smoothing down castings or cleaning up weld joints, a 24-grit wheel may be right. One of 36 grit, slightly finer, will also remove stock rapidly and is useful for shaping tools like lathe bits, which may call for grinding away a good-sized chunk of metal. For reshaping edges, a medium-fine 60-grit wheel is recommended, and this is a good stone for general coarse sharpening. For fine-edged tools like boring bits, small twist drills, wood chisels—and for finish grinding of larger tools —a 100-grit wheel is useful. You might want a 200-grit wheel for cutlery, carving tools, scrapers and other fine edges, although you could grind these on a coarser stone and finish them on a good bench stone.

Alundum (aluminum oxide) wheels are right for the majority of sharpening jobs. But use Crystolon (silicon carbide) wheels for sharpening tungsten-carbide tipped lathe bits, masonry bits, and circular saws. Wheels of green Crystolon (technically known as 39 Crystolon) are best for such cemented-carbide tools.

Grinding-wheel shapes. The most common wheel is the straight wheel, a plain disk usually ½" to 1" thick, with a hole to fit the shaft or spindle of the grinding head (Figure 3). All grinding should be done on the periphery or edge of such a wheel. Grinding on the side is frowned upon because it may eventually groove or undercut the wheel enough to dangerously weaken it.

This objection is overcome in straight and flaring cup wheels (Figure 3). All grinding on these should be done on the rim face. Wear on this will not weaken such wheels. There is also the steel reinforced wheel, a ring-shaped one cemented to a steel backing disk. This provides a wide grinding face for sharpening twist drills and other work that can handily be done on the side of a wheel.

Mounted wheels (Figure 4) come in a variety of shapes, usually in small

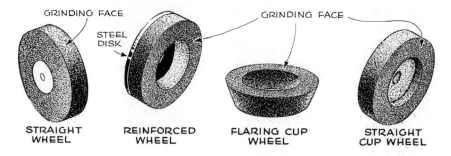

Fig. 3. Standard grinding wheel shapes. Only the edge of the straight wheel should be used for grinding. The other types are used with a side as the grinding surface.

Fig. 4. Mounted grinding wheels, usually under 2" in size, are used in electric drills or small hand grinders.

sizes up to 2". These wheels are fixed on mandrels (shafts) that may be mounted in ordinary drill chucks or in those of small hand grinders. They are useful for special jobs such as touching up dull taps and dies.

Grinders are of two main types: those with a built-in motor, the wheels being mounted directly on the two ends of the motor shaft; and those to be belt driven from a separate motor. The first kind are more expensive, but also more compact and convenient, having no pulleys to work loose or wear, and no belt to require tightening or replacement. However, belt-driven grinder heads are perfectly practical, and a good one with ball bearings and two 6" wheels can be bought for about $13. If you buy a belt-driven machine, it is your own responsibility to select drive pulleys that will give it the correct spindle speed.

Belt-driven grinder head must be powered by a separate motor hitched to pulley concealed between the grinding wheels. To give the grinder the correct speed, it is necessary to select the right pulley for the motor. *Courtesy Montgomery Ward.*

Bench grinder with a built-in motor is standard tool in many woodworking shops. For safety it should have features shown here: big flanges on the wheel arbor, guard and end covers for the wheels, tool rests, and spark shields of shatterproof glass. *Courtesy Black & Decker.*

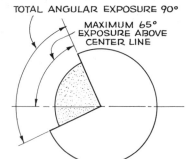

TOTAL ANGULAR EXPOSURE 90°

MAXIMUM 65°
EXPOSURE ABOVE
CENTER LINE

Fig. 5. To protect the user from flying fragments, the wheel guard of a power grinder should expose only 90 degrees of the wheel, 65 degrees above the center line.

Though simple as machines go, a grinder should meet certain important requirements. One of these is a substantial guard that completely surrounds the wheel except for a 90- degree segment where the work is done. The guard must be sturdy enough to withstand wheel breakage and so protect anyone nearby from flying fragments. No more than 65 degrees of wheel exposure should be above the horizontal center line (Figure 5). (For some special jobs, the American Standard Safety Code does permit more than 90 degrees of wheel exposure—up to 60 degrees below the center line, but no more than 65 above.)

A guard adequate for one wheel size may fail to provide protection with a smaller wheel, or even for the same wheel as it wears smaller. Figure 6 shows how this condition can develop, increasing the exposure angle so much that shards of a breaking wheel could fly at the operator. Some guards are adjustable and can be moved back to compensate for this. Others have an adjustable tongue that can be lowered for the same purpose (Figure 7).

A good grinder should also have a sturdy adjustable tool rest. This should be tightened with its innermost edge no more than ⅛″ from the wheel face so that work cannot slip between the rest and the wheel, an accident that could cause jamming and wheel breakage.

Shatterproof eye shields are mounted on some grinders, and available as optional extras on others. They are well worth having.

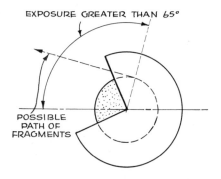

Fig. 6. When the wheel wears smaller, and exposure is greater than 65 degrees above the center line, the user is in danger of being struck by fragments.

Fig. 7. On some grinders, increased wheel exposure can be counteracted by an adjustable tongue which can be moved down to protect the user.

SAFETY HINTS. Though grinding wheels are safe if properly mounted and used, they are subject to breakage if dropped or abused. Before mounting any wheel, old or new, inspect it for cracks. Then hold it on a pencil thrust through the center hole and rap it gently with a screwdriver handle or a wooden mallet at the points shown in Figure 8. A good vitrified or silicate wheel should have a clear metallic ring when struck. If such a wheel has a dull tone, it is probably cracked and should be discarded—preferably broken up so that it won't be used by mistake. (Wheels with rubber or other organic bonds do not ring, so this test is not valid for them.)

Fig. 8. Testing a grinding wheel for cracks. A good vitrified or silicate wheel should emit a clear metallic ring when struck.

Wheels may have holes larger than your spindle. Usually bushings are included to reduce the hole to certain standard sizes. These bushings are perfectly acceptable so long as they don't interfere with correct seating of the mounting flanges. A wheel must be gripped on the flange diameter, not by the bushing.

The flanges of good grinding heads are recessed (Figure 9) so that only the outer part of them makes contact with the wheel. Don't use ordinary washers as flanges. Tighten the arbor or spindle nut only enough to drive the wheel without slippage. Figure 10 shows the possible effect of overtightening. It can distort the flanges and drastically reduce the contact area.

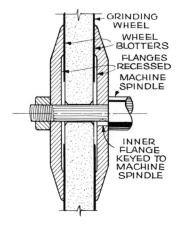

Fig. 9. Recessed flanges contact grinding wheel only on the outer part. Blotters provide a compressible face between flanges and wheel.

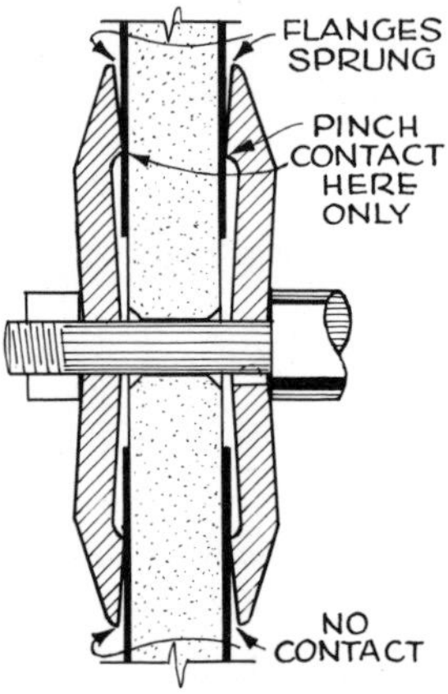

Fig. 10. Overtightening flanges distorts them, reduces contact area against the wheel.

The paper disks around the shaft holes on grinding wheels, called *blotters*, aren't there just to hold on the print, though wheel specifications usually are marked on them. The blotters provide a compressible facing between the wheel proper and the metal mounting flanges. They should be big enough to fulfill this purpose, covering the entire flange area and a bit more.

Should a blotter be torn, peel off every scrap from both the wheel and the flange, to which some may be stuck. Use abrasive paper on a wood block, if necessary, to shave clinging fragments off the wheel. Cut a new blotter out of *thin* blotting paper and glue it to the wheel. It is wise to transfer label markings to the new blotter if possible.

Wheels are marked for the maximum speed at which they may be run. *Never drive them at higher speeds.* It is safe, though a trifle less efficient, to run them at lower speeds. Think twice any time you mount a new wheel, especially if it is larger than the old. Check the wheel label and the spindle speed of your grinder. If it is belt driven, you can find its speed after determining the motor speed (usually marked on its name plate) and measuring the two drive pulleys.

The formula is simple. Multiply the motor speed by the diameter of the motor pulley. Then divide the product by the diameter of the pulley on the grinder. The result is the speed of the grinder shaft.

Wear your goggles. They'll do you no good hung on a nail or left in a drawer. Unless the grinder has big, shatterproof eye shields, goggles should be worn every time you switch it on. Don't make the mistake of thinking only sparks are dangerous. Many flying particles are invisible. Nor are ordinary eyeglasses a substitute for goggles.

Keep wheels in trim. When a grinding wheel begins to get loaded, it can sometimes be cleaned by holding a piece of a broken wheel against it as it runs. Even better is a Crystolon wheel dressing stick. Such a stick, or a somewhat costlier Bear wheel dresser, can also true a wheel that has worn eccentric, and even reshape the face for special grinding operations.

Star-wheel dressers have a husky handle at the end of which star-shaped steel wheels, somewhat like the rowel on a spur, rotate on a shaft or on ball bearings. The handle has two projections at this end, which are to be hooked over the front of the tool rest. As the other end of the handle is raised, the star wheels are forced into the rotating grinding wheel. A few seconds are enough to dress the wheel, the tool being traversed across its face in the process.

This apparently brutal method of wheel dressing is both safe and effective. If sparking is heavy, it is a sign that the star wheels are being ground, instead of dressing the wheel. The remedy is to apply more pressure.

Deluxe wheel dressers have diamonds mounted in a suitable handle or mount, for use by hand or for mounting in a tool holder. Diamond dressers are worth their price in industrial precision grinding but are hardly necessary for amateur or home sharpening wheels.

Glazed wheels should be dressed promptly. If glazing occurs again and again, check possible reasons for it. Grinding soft metals such as brass will load and eventually glaze a wheel. Ordinarily, only ferrous metals should be ground. Glazing may occur because a wheel is running too rapidly for the work in hand, even if it is operating within speed specifications. Try a lower speed. Finally, the wheel may be too hard. A softer grade that breaks down more quickly may be less prone to glazing.

IMPROVISED GRINDERS. The wide availability of ¼″-hp. motors that can be salvaged from washing machines and other appliances offers tempting possibilities. Some such motors have two speeds that can be changed by flipping a switch. Even the common 1,750-r.p.m. motor will make a serviceable grinder if correctly fitted with 6″ or 7″ wheels. An arbor that can be mounted on the shaft with a setscrew, and has a threaded section with a fixed and a loose flange for the grinding wheel, makes a simple wheel mount. See that the flanges grip the wheel blotters properly.

Fitting an adequate guard and tool rest is more difficult. A boxlike guard of ¾″ plywood, assembled with glue and wood screws, should be strong enough to contain a breaking wheel. The guard must be fastened down securely with brackets, bolts, and nuts, not in some more casual and weaker

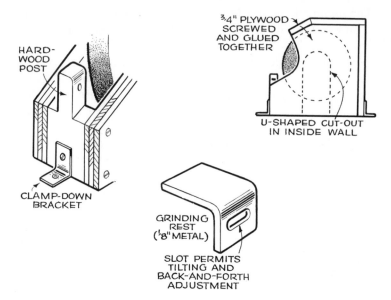

Fig. 11. A grinder improvised from a ¼-h.p. motor should have a plywood guard. Tool rest can be fashioned of iron plate and held in place with a bolt and wing nut.

fashion. A tool rest can be bent up of ⅛″ iron plate and held in adjustment with a bolt and wing nut (Figure 11).

One national mail-order house offers a grinding attachment to fit any motor with a ½″ shaft. The attachment includes a wheel arbor, a guard, a tool rest, and an eye shield. For roughly $8 it converts a salvaged split-phase motor into a reasonably useful one-wheel grinder.

A word of caution: *don't* try to use a salvaged vacuum-cleaner motor or any other "universal" type having two brushes and a commutator. These rev up to tremendous speed unless they have a built-in load such as gearing or the air impeller of a vacuum cleaner. Without a load, they can reach velocities high enough to shatter a grinding wheel by centrifugal force. Ordinary split-phase alternating-current motors, the kind used in refrigerators, dryers and washing machines, usually have their speed marked on the nameplate and can be relied upon not to exceed it.

A power hone is a fine-grit wheel driven at a comparatively low speed and lubricated during use with cup grease or Vaseline. It can put an excellent edge on cutlery, chisels, and other fine-edged tools. One version of this machine, no longer being made, had a vertical grinding wheel running at a suitable speed, with gearing that drove a horizontal honing wheel much more slowly (Figure 12). The wheel had a square hole engaging a square-ended shaft, and was simply flipped over to change from a fine-grit side to a coarse-grit side or vice versa.

Ingenious mechanics may find it possible to build such a machine for themselves. The honing wheel may run at 600 to 1,000 r.p.m., preferably in a

Fig. 12. Power hone geared to a grinding wheel is an aid in putting the finishing touches on a sharpening job. The type shown here is not manufactured any more, but an ingenious mechanic could build one.

tray or recess so that it won't fling grease out. To avoid having a spindle and nut protrude, the wheel might be cemented to a backing plate. A horizontal bar above the wheel might hold an adjustable tilting tool rest.

Belt sanders will sharpen a number of things, including scissors, axes, tin snips, and knives. For some sharpening, it is desirable to have the belt running away from the edge instead of toward it. The easy way to achieve this is to stand at the back of the belt sander instead of in the usual position. Though a stationary or bench sander is most convenient, even a portable one can be used if securely fastened in an upside-down position. The aluminum-oxide belts used for sanding wood are quite suitable for sharpening. Be sure to wear goggles, because there is nothing else between your eyes and flying particles.

A ribbon sander using 1″-wide sanding belts is also a versatile sharpening machine. The belts are comparatively cheap and come in several grits. Their

Ribbon sander using a 1″-wide belt does much the same work as a conventional grinding wheel of tremendous size. Because contact area is so long, the work stays cool, belt clogging is reduced. Belts are cheap, come in many grits.

Sharpening disc for use with drills of 1,700 to 2,500 r.p.m. does a fast, efficient job on axes, hoes, rotary-mower blades, etc. Made of rigid neoprene, it is coated with 24-grit aluminum oxide.

length makes them both cool-cutting and long-wearing. A fine grit belt does the nearest thing to a honing job, especially if it is lubricated.

An early version of this machine, called the Bandsander, was made by Mead Specialties Company, of Chicago. The ribbon sander has been updated recently in a more rugged form by Rockwell Manufacturing Company, makers of several other fine woodworking tools.

Sharpening with an electric drill. The ubiquitous electric drill can supply the muscle but not the accuracy for a variety of off-hand sharpening chores. How well it does will depend on your own eyes and steadiness of hand, and the eyes must—repeat *must*—be protected with adequate goggles.

The grinding element may be a 4″ wheel mounted on a suitable adapter, a mounted wheel fastened in the chuck, or a rubber-backed sanding disk with aluminum-oxide paper on it. Take great care to check grinding wheels for cracks before mounting them, for the absence of a guard makes their use hazardous.

Radial-arm saw equipped with a grinding wheel does an efficient job of sharpening a variety of tools. A machinist's vise, mounted on a square of plywood screwed to the runner in the table slot, holds tools at the proper grinding angle. For precision hollow grinding of chisels, hand plane irons, jointer and planer knives (top, right), merely clamp the tool in the vise and pull the saw carriage across, lowering the wheel as sharpening progresses. With a simple jig (center), you can sharpen twist drills down to the smaller sizes. Just grasp the bit in the thumb and forefinger, and with the vise turned to about 60 degrees in relation to the grinding wheel, move the bit against the wheel while holding the lip being ground at about 10:30 o'clock. Treat both lips the same. To sharpen turning chisels, roll them inside vise-held curtain ring (bottom). These techniques developed by William G. Waggoner.

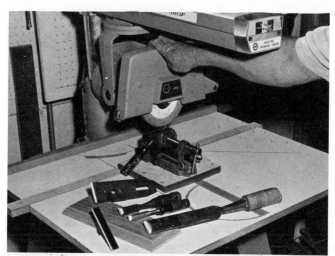

Not long ago the Stanley Works introduced a useful sharpening disk of neoprene impregnated with 24-grit aluminum oxide. Its shank fits into the drill chuck, and the disk can safely withstand speeds far higher than those of the average electric drill. Designed for sharpening garden tools, axes, and rotary-mower blades, this coarse-grit disk works so fast you'll do well to practice on a bar of scrap steel before tackling a valuable edged tool. At the risk of being repetitive, it must be emphasized that goggles must be worn.

GRINDING-WHEEL REMINDERS

HANDLE wheels carefully. Never use one that has been dropped.

INSPECT a wheel every time you mount it. Apply ring test.

CHECK maximum speed rating on the blotter. Don't exceed it.

USE an approved bushing if center hole is too big for the shaft.

NEVER force a wheel onto a spindle.

CLEAN off blotters and mounting flanges before you mount a wheel.

DON'T tighten spindle nuts excessively.

LET newly mounted wheels run a full minute before use.

STAND clear whenever a grinder is started up.

DON'T grind on the side of a straight wheel.

WEAR goggles every time you grind.

CHAPTER THREE

YOUR YARD AND GARDEN TOOLS

That old wheeze "dull as a hoe" should never have started, for by rights a hoe shouldn't be dull. Try sharpening an old one and see what a difference it makes in use. Even spades are better for sharpening. They'll cut through sod and soil more easily, do a better job of edging. Grass snips will cut the first time you close them, instead of the third or fourth, if they're as sharp as good shears.

Though an engine furnishes the muscle power in a power mower and so may mask the need for sharpening, the difference will show on your lawn. A sharp rotary-mower blade will cut the grass cleanly instead of merely beating part of it down, and one pass will do a better job than two with a dull blade. As for toothed tools like pruning saws and electric hedge clippers, a few minutes of struggling with dull ones will convince anyone of the merits of timely sharpening.

There are just two main rules to keep in mind for sharpening garden tools—and they apply to most other things too. (1) Sharpen as nearly as you can to the same bevel angles the tool had when new. (2) Don't take off more metal than you have to.

HOES AND SPADES are among the easiest yard tools to sharpen. You don't need a grinding wheel for them. Either a 10″ mill bastard file or a coarse silicon-carbide stone (such as the Crystolon Utility File) will do a good job.

There is only one bevel on a blade of a hoe, and its angle may be from 45 to 85 degrees to the flat of the blade (Figure 1). The short 85-degree angle is sturdier and better for general work. The longer 45-degree angle provides a keener edge for weed chopping or sod cutting, but won't stand up as long.

Although a file or a handled stone can be used outdoors, you're likely to do a better sharpening job with the tool locked in a vise at a convenient working height. Conventionally, the edge bevel on a hoe is on the bottom, away from the handle (Figure 1) but some gardeners prefer it on the inside instead. If you are right-handed, start filing or stoning at the right-hand end of

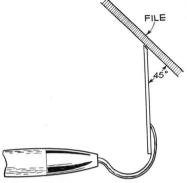

FILE

45°

Fig. 1. Edge bevel on a hoe is usually on the bottom.

the blade, holding the file at the correct angle and slanted toward the left. As you push it forward, traverse it to the left also so that the full length of the edge is filed at each stroke. Lift the file on the return stroke. Keep the edge of a hoe straight.

Sharpening will take less time if you are deliberate and accurate, making every stroke count. Be sure to maintain the same angle constantly; if you rock the file, you'll round the bevel and probably produce a poor edge. A few correct strokes will accomplish more than a lot of haphazard ones. After forming the bevel, hold the file *flat* against the other side and remove the wire edge with a few light strokes.

For weeding in tight spots, you can sharpen the sides as well as the bottom of the blade. The corners will stand up to service a bit better if they are slightly rounded. You may want to try a double-purpose hoe. Sharpen the usual edge at 85 degrees for tough going, the sides at 45 degrees for nipping out stubborn small weeds.

On a spade (or a shovel, which will also work better for having a sharp edge) the bevel should be on the inside or upper surface of the blade. A flat file or stone will sharpen even the concave blade of a shovel. You can also use a sharpening disk in an electric drill (wear goggles for this). It's not necessary to remove the wire edge.

Begin filing a hoe at the right-hand end of the blade, holding the file at the correct angle and slanted toward the left. File on the push stroke only, lifting the file on the return stroke. For weeding in tight places, sharpen the sides as well.

A spade or a shovel will give better service if its edge is kept sharp. File the bevel on the inside edge.

SCYTHES, SICKLES, AND GRASS WHIPS. Long-handled tools of this kind are awkward to grind, and the curved blades may require removal of the guard and tool rest. This may take longer than doing the whole job with a file or a handstone. The difficulty of applying curved blades to the wheel at the correct angle increases the risk of grinding damage. Save wheel grinding, therefore, for the time scythe or sickle blades are badly nicked.

For effective work, however, these tools can profitably be whetted right on the job, so it will pay to carry a stone with you.

Stand a scythe on its handle, the blade nearly horizontal. Starting at the snath (handle) end, hold an oval-sectioned scythestone at 10 degrees to the flat of the blade. Stroke the stone downward, while traversing it a short way toward the point. Whet on the down stroke only, lifting the stone on the return stroke. Use oil or water on the stone if any is available.

Repeat these overlapping strokes until the entire blade length is whetted. Then turn the blade around to sharpen the opposite bevel, also at 10 degrees, which will give the edge an included angle of 20 degrees. (Some users prefer a finer one of 10 degrees.)

Whetting across the blade this way leaves a series of microscopic teeth on the edge, which some users deem desirable. But another way of whetting a scythe, recommended by a manufacturer of scythestones, is to rest the stone on the raised backbone of the blade as well as on its edge, and stroke in an arc from heel to tip without moving the stone down at all (Figure 2). This has the advantage of maintaining the bevel angle automatically. Whetting should be done on both sides of the blade, of course.

Once a scythe blade is rusted, nicked, or very dull, it may be necessary to recondition it on a grinder or a wet grindstone. Removing a single bolt usually

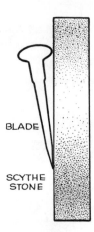

Fig. 2. Sharpen a scythe by resting the stone on the raised backbone of the blade and stroking the full length of the blade, from heel to toe, as shown in the photo.

frees the blade from the handle. Try positioning the blade against the wheel while it is stationary to get the proper angle, holding the blade with the point up, tang end down. Start grinding at the tang end, using light pressure, and moving the blade down toward the tip. Take care, when approaching this end, not to let it catch on the wheel.

Grind equal bevels on both sides. Some users believe the wire edge left by grinding adds to the cutting ability of the blade. If you want to remove it, a few strokes with a handstone will do so. Occasional hand whetting should keep a scythe sharp for some time before grinding is again necessary. If you do much sharpening of this kind, you may want to buy a special dual-cone sickle grinding wheel, which can be used for scythes too.

Sickles usually have a single bevel and so are sharpened on one side only. You can use an oval-sectioned scythestone or a handled stone such as the Crystolon Home and Garden Sharpener (Figure 3). Remove the wire edge by whetting the other side lightly, holding the stone flat against it.

Fig. 3. Sharpening a sickle with handled Crystolon stone. Sickles, which usually have a single bevel, are sharpened on one side only.

Grass whips, which let you cut high grass with a golf swing, may have the blade integral with the shaft or bolted to it. The bevel may be on top or on the bottom of the blade, and the edge straight or serrated. This tool is a natural for file sharpening. Even if in bad condition, the edge can be filed straight and then resharpened.

However, when the bevel is on top, the shaft may interfere with filing at the requisite angle (Figure 4). In that case, unscrew the nuts holding the blade, and fasten it with flathead wood screws to a piece of wood, the blade bevels up (there are usually two bevels, so that the whip will cut on both forward and back strokes). Clamp the wood to a bench or table edge, or in a vise, for sharpening.

File at the original bevel angle, which is usually 25 degrees to the flat of the blade. Remove the wire edge on nonserrated blades with a few file strokes flat across the other side.

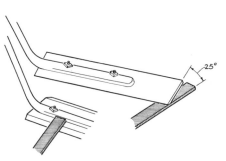 

Fig. 4. Filing a grass whip is easy if the bevel is on the underside. If it's on top and the file hits the shaft, remove the blade, fasten it to a wood block and clamp it in a vise, as in the photo.

BRUSH HOOK AND MACHETE. Because of the reverse curve of a brush hook, a scythestone or a handled sharpening stone is called for. It's easiest to stroke the stone lengthwise of the blade, but where the hook occurs, swing it in an arc to maintain the same bevel angle throughout. Whet both sides of the blade much as you would a scythe (Figure 5).

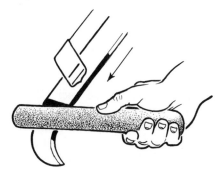

Fig. 5. To sharpen a brush hook with a scythestone, stroke along the straight part of the blade, swinging the stone in an arc and keeping the same angle at the curved section.

The straight blade of a machete can be sharpened with the same sort of stone or with a disk-like axe stone. This round stone is used with a circular motion, being tilted to match the bevel angle. Hold the machete down firmly, and whet with overlapping circular strokes, starting at the heel of the blade.

SHARPENING GARDEN SHEARS. These tools range from grass snips to rugged pruning shears, and usually have scissors-like blades. They are easiest to sharpen if the blades can be taken apart and treated separately, but this is not always possible.

Grass snips having a riveted pivot bolt are an example of this. The blades won't open far enough to permit sharpening on a wheel, and they may be so hard as to make filing impracticable. Try a thin file first, however, if the blades are in poor condition and much metal has to be removed. If you haven't a vise, brace one blade against a table or bench edge. Hold a file or a small hand-stone at 10 to 12 degrees from the horizontal (making the blade bevel between 80 and 78 degrees). Note that the blade bevel slopes away from the inner blade surfaces (Figure 6).

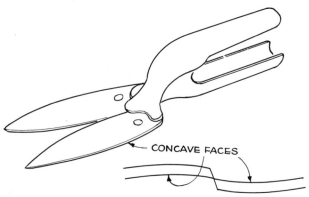

CONCAVE FACES

Fig. 6. Grass snips have blades with concave faces; the bevel angle slopes away from the inner blade surfaces.

ABRASIVE RIBBON

OPEN BLADES

BACKING PLATEN

TABLE TILTED

WOOD BLOCK

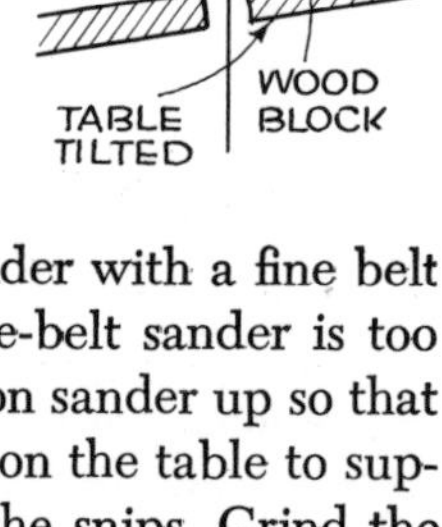

Fig. 7. Cross section of snips being sharpened on a ribbon sander. The wood block supports the blade and allows clearance for handle.

Snips can be sharpened successfully on a ribbon sander with a fine belt on it (Figure 7). The backing plate of an ordinary wide-belt sander is too thick to get between the blades. Tilt the table of the ribbon sander up so that it slopes down toward the belt. Place a thick wood block on the table to support the blade and provide clearance for the handle of the snips. Grind the right-hand blade with the handle of the snips to the left and up, the left-hand

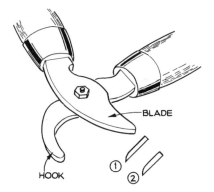

Fig. 8. Curved-blade pruning shears. If the blade has a double bevel (1), it will cut more easily if you round off the juncture (2).

BLADE

HOOK ① ②

To sharpen the blade of pruning shears on the job, spread the handles apart and rest the ends on the ground. File *toward* the cutting edge. Only one edge usually needs sharpening.

blade with the handle also to the left, but down (which is where the block comes in). It's not necessary to stone off any feather edges; closing the snips will break them off.

The inside blade surfaces of good snips (those facing each other when the blades are closed) are forged or ground concave. They should not be touched when sharpening is done.

Straight-blade garden shears can be opened farther than grass snips and thus can be sharpened like scissors—on a wheel, a bench stone, or a belt sander (See Chapter 4). Check bevel angles carefully before starting to grind, for the bevels are often narrow and it may be difficult to see which way they slant. It's worth remembering that the bevel always slopes away from the inside blade surface toward the outer surface. Wipe grinding dust off after sharpening, and oil the pivot.

Curved-blade pruning or lopping shears, and tree trimmers, have a single convex-edged blade working against a hook or a cutting bar, which is square-edged and not sharpened (Figure 8). For on-the-job sharpening, you can spread the handles wide, rest them on the ground, and file the blade as shown in the photo.

For a better job, take out the pivot bolt and separate the blade from the hook. You can then use a flat file or a stone to dress the bevel on the blade. This can also be done on a grinding wheel or a belt sander, but don't ever hold the curved blade still against either wheel or belt. Keep it moving to maintain the curve of the edge and avoid grinding flat spaces on it. Remove the feather edge with a handstone held flat against the other side of the blade. (It's safest to do this by hand. A wheel or belt may impair the flatness of the surface, which is important to good cutting action.)

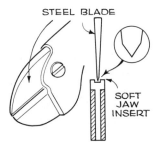

Fig. 9. Steel blade of rose cutters, which has a steep edge bevel, can be sharpened with an oilstone in lengthwise passes.

Some shear blades have a single bevel of about 25 degrees all the way to the cutting edge. Others have a second, slightly steeper bevel near the edge. You'll get easier wood penetration if you round off the apex between the two bevels. If there is any play in the pivot, it is important to tighten the pivot nut or take other measures to minimize such play. A new pivot bolt may be indicated. In shears that have a soft-metal anvil, cutting action is improved by replacing the anvil when it's worn. The hook type of cutter bar should be square at the edge (at 90 degrees to the blade) and not rounded. If it is rounded by normal wear, square it up with a half-round file.

Fig. 10. Sharpening an axe on a grinding wheel to produce a convex bevel on the edge.

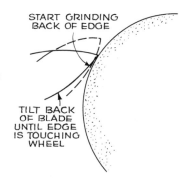

Rose cutters, small enough to use in one hand, have a single straight-edged blade working against a soft cutter bar (Figure 9). The hard-working blade has a very narrow and fairly steep edge bevel, befitting its job. Use a magnifying glass, if necessary, to ascertain the bevel angle and to dress it with a handstone. A few lengthwise passes with a small pocket stone on each of the two bevels should suffice to sharpen the edge.

HATCHETS, AXES, AND ADZES. When these tools are intended for splitting, they have a short blade bevel and plenty of steel back of the edge. For peeling, trimming, and cutting, the bevel may be longer, the blade thinner and more tapered. These characteristics should not be altered in grinding, but recognized so that the tool will be sharpened for its intended purpose. Even a short bevel or a heavy, convex blade section is no excuse for dullness. Axes and hatchets should be given a finely whetted, keen edge.

These tools can be ground on a wet or a dry wheel. Let an axe touch the grinding wheel first an inch from the edge (Figure 10). Swing the blade from side to side constantly so as to grind the full width, gradually tilting the back of the axe head up to bring the grinding contact nearer the edge. This should form a full-width convex bevel. (A concave or hollow-ground bevel would require the removal of far too much metal, and weaken the blade.) Dip the blade in water occasionally, or stop grinding to let it air-cool frequently. Take extra care when grinding near the edge, when the metal can overheat more quickly.

Fig. 11. When grinding an axe on a belt sander, rock the blade back and forth, as shown by the arrows, to produce a rounded bevel. For blades requiring a flat bevel (rotary-mower blades, hatchets) hold the work steady.

Having ground one bevel to the edge, flip the axe over and grind the other the same way. Take care to keep the edge straight or curved, as the case may be. The work can be done on a belt sander (Figure 11), but it is best to have the belt traveling away from the edge, not into it.

If an axe edge is battered and nicked, trace its overall curve on paper as a guide to reshaping it. This can be done on a grinding wheel or with a file; some experts prefer the latter. Grind or file away all nicks, shaping the new contour to the traced profile. File, grind, or sand away any scratches on the surface of the blade near the edge, for these can be crack starters. So can edge crimps caused by impact.

Fig. 12. Circular strokes with a lubricated combination oilstone whet an axe to a sharp edge. Start with the coarse side of the stone and finish with the fine.

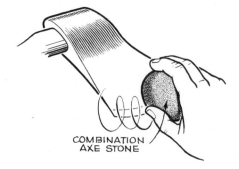

COMBINATION
AXE STONE

After grinding, use a stone for whetting to a good edge. Keep the stone wet with oil, kerosene, or water. Move it with a circular motion (Figure 12), overlapping the circles as you work the length of the cutting edge, dressing first one side of the blade and then the other. If you have a combination stone, start with the coarse side and finish with the fine. Don't pronounce the edge really sharp unless it will cut a clean slit in cloth laid flat on a board, or whittle shavings off an edge as easily as a keen pocketknife.

Hatchets usually have a slimmer, more tapering blade and a well-defined flat edge bevel (Figure 13). Sharpen them as nearly to the original bevels as you can. Small hatchets may be moved across a bench stone, instead of moving the stone against the tool. If the edge is curved, rock the blade so as to stone all parts of the edge equally without producing flat spots in it.

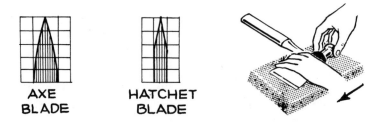

**AXE
BLADE**   **HATCHET
BLADE**

Fig. 13. Comparison between the edge bevels of typical axe and hatchet blades. Hatchet blade can be whetted on a bench stone, or, as above, on a piece of aluminum oxide cloth (about 120 grit) tacked over a block.

THE MATTOCK, a heavy-duty tool, will also do better work if it is sharpened occasionally. Its main bevel is on the inside or underside of the wide end of the blade. A mattock may be too hard to file, but an aluminum-oxide belt on a portable belt sander will sharpen it nicely. So will an abrasive disk in an electric drill. Be sure to wear goggles.

Hold or clamp the mattock head down firmly. If you can remove the handle, the head may be bolted down as shown in the photo. The point should not be sharp, but rounded to an area about ⅛" square to withstand impact (Figure 14). When badly chipped or deeply nicked, a mattock becomes a job for a blacksmith shop. There it can be heated, reshaped at both ends, grinder-sharpened and retempered.

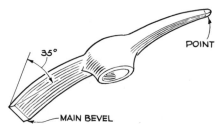

Fig. 14. Grind the main bevel of a mattock to about a 35-degree angle, then round off the tip to about $\frac{1}{8}$"-square area to avoid breakage.

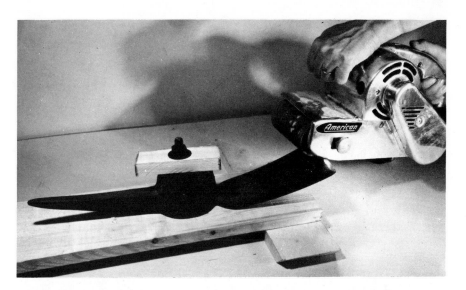

Belt sander is the best choice for sharpening a mattock. Bolt the head to a board and clamp the board to the workbench. Used as shown, the belt splice won't snag on the edge of the tool.

HEDGE CLIPPERS. The long-bladed manual type typically have a 60-degree bevel angle. As the blades can be opened widely, they can be sharpened with a file, on a wheel or belt sander, or with a sharpening disk in an electric drill. Use the latter with caution. Fitting a wood strip on the blade, as shown in the photo, is a good way to check on the bevel angle as you are sharpening. It tips you off to grinding action in time to avoid distressing errors. A file or a hand-stone is slower but safer, a belt or ribbon sander speedy and accurate. For filling or stoning, clamp one blade at a time between wood strips in a vise.

Whatever you use, the sharpening action should be across the cutting edge, perpendicular to the plane of the blade, rather than along it. This kind of sharpening leaves tiny serrations on the edge that nip into stalks or twigs as you shear them, and prevent them from sliding along the blades.

Never remove more material than necessary. Shear blades are bowed and twisted so that the contact point between them moves toward the tip as they close. If you remove too much metal, you will destroy the contact pressure and the shears will never be the same again. Don't change the leading-edge bevel. If blade edges are not alike (as on some new models) don't try to make them so.

Power hedge clippers sever twigs between beveled teeth on a recipro-cating blade, and unbeveled teeth on a stationary comb. Unless the latter has been damaged, only the cutter blade should need attention. If you remove it, take care to note how it fits, and the position of all spring or other washers that hold it against the comb. Clamp the blade in a vise, preferably with wood pads on each side, the bevel side of the teeth facing you. However, cutter teeth can be filed or stoned without dismantling the clippers.

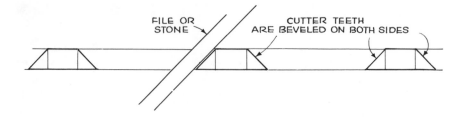

Fig. 15. Filing the beveled cutter teeth of power hedge clippers.

Holding a 7" or 8" slim taper file at the bevel angle on one side of a tooth, file on the push stroke only (Figure 15). Take care not to file the next adjacent edge at this angle. A few strokes on each bevel should suffice to remove nicks and turn up a fine wire edge on the back. File both the bevels on each tooth, keeping the points centered. However, don't file any tooth more than necessary, nor fret if the teeth aren't all alike. (Unlike saw teeth, each does its own job instead of following in the track of the others.) Finally, rub a fine flat file or a stone flat on the other side of the blade to remove the wire edges.

Wooden strip, slotted to fit on the blade of hedge clippers, serves as a visual guide for maintaining the correct angle while filing. Take light strokes *across* the cutting edge to leave tiny serrations which catch on stalks, prevent blades from slipping.

Should the comb teeth be rounded off at the clipping edge, they won't back up the cutter teeth properly. Use a mill file to dress the tooth sides at 90 degrees. Shape the gullets (rounded bottoms) with a round file.

Clean off all filing chips and sharpening dust thoroughly from the blade and comb. Then apply a thin film of oil to the blade and comb surfaces, and reassemble the tool.

Keep a rotary-mower blade sharp by filing after every other mowing. Hold the tip with your left hand and touch up the bevel on the upper edge with short strokes of the file.

An abrasive sharpening disk in an electric drill offers a quick means of grinding a rotary-mower blade. It's wise to clamp a wood strip in front of the blade as a gauge in grinding a 30-degree bevel angle. Do not touch the up-tilted rear lip of the blade.

ROTARY-MOWER BLADES. This popular type of mower is easy to sharpen, and the chore is rewarding because you can see the difference it makes. Even a dull rotary-mower blade cuts, but it doesn't cut clean—a number of blades of grass will escape it at every turn, and come up standing to give the lawn a ragged look. Some mower manufacturers advise removing and sharpening the blade after every third mowing. You may do just as well, however, by file-dressing the blade after every second mowing, without removing it.

Run your mower fuel tank nearly empty to avoid spillage when you tip the mower over for sharpening. If the engine has an oil-bath filter, take this off. Most important, remove the spark plug. *Never touch the blade of a rotary mower unless the plug is out.* Cantankerous and hard starting as these little engines sometimes are, they have been known to start up when somebody pulled the blade around by hand.

It may be tempting to simply pull off the spark-plug cable. But unless the cable is securely tied back, it may spring back to its accustomed position and touch the plug. Don't risk it. Removing the plug removes all accidental-starting hazard, gives you a chance to inspect the plug and clean it if necessary, and by relieving engine compression makes it much easier to position the blade for sharpening.

Turn the blade to a handy working position, hold one tip with your left hand, and file with your right. The bevels—one at each end of the blade—are on the top side, so the file must work between the blade and the housing. Special rotary-mower files are made short so that they won't hit the mower housing when used this way. Use moderate pressure on the forward stroke, sliding the file slowly sidewise to blend the bevel its full length. Lift the file on the back strokes. Work slowly, keeping count of the strokes, and judge the keenness of the edge by feel. Turn the blade 180 degrees and file the opposite edge, counting strokes again so that you will file equal amounts from both ends of the blade and so maintain its balance. (Imbalance can damage the motor.)

Since balance is extremely important, it is wise to remove the blade occasionally both for resharpening and balancing. If the original bevel is lost, regrind it to 30 degrees. Should there be a few deep nicks, don't grind back the entire edge to remove them. Round any V-nicks to a U-shape, so that the sharp apex won't be a crack-starting point.

Should you find any cracks, however, don't take risks by trying to salvage the blade. Discard it at once. A cracked blade may fly apart at any time.

For accurate balancing, push a cork or a plug with an accurately centered hole in it into the shaft hole. Thread a string through the plug, or push a knitting needle or other straight wire through it and support it on the opened jaws of a vice to check blade balance. (Don't try to balance a blade by hanging it on a nail, which will be off-center in the shaft hole.)

Opposite each edge, the blade of a rotary mower has an uptilt or lip. Leave this alone when balancing the blade; remove metal only along the cutting-edge bevel. The upslanting lip creates an upward air blast that holds the grass upright for mowing. This air lift is vital to good cutting, so do nothing to alter or impair the turned-up lips.

One relatively new type of rotary mower has a plastic disk to which are affixed small cutting blades. Pivoted on their mounting pins, these blades are held out by centrifugal force with sufficient rigidity to cut grass, but swing back if they hit a stone or a nail in the grass. The blades can be removed individually and may be resharpened or replaced as required.

REEL-TYPE MOWERS. The cutting reels of this mower have spiral blades that are almost impossible to sharpen without special equipment, for the bevel angle changes at every point along its length. Nevertheless, there are some things you can do to make this kind of mower cut better. (If it is a power mower, be sure to remove the engine plug.)

First of all, if it cuts on one side better than on the other, it may merely need adjustment of the bed knife. This is a straight, stationary blade against which the reel turns with minute clearance. Impact with obstacles may have misaligned the bed knife so that there is excessive clearance at one end. Two adjusting screws at each end, or in some models two nuts on each of two eye bolts, can tilt the bed knife one way or the other to set it nearer or farther from the reel blades. Clearance should be less than the thickness of a newspaper sheet; a sheet of cigarette paper is often suggested as a gauge for setting the bed knife, but you can judge it as well by moving the knife up until

By turning a reel mower upside down, it is usually possible to sharpen the bed knife without removing it. On this Sears Craftsman mower, the bed knife is square edged. It was whetted by sliding a small stone along it, with heavy thumb pressure to keep it in full contact and avoid rocking. As whetting progressed, the reel was slowly turned to keep its blade out of the way.

the reel blades just scrape the bed knife, and then backing it off very slightly.

Sharpening the bed knife alone may be all the mower requires. Use a stone or a medium-cutting flat file on the bevel, which is on the underside of the blade. The edge must be straight as well as sharp. If it requires much work, you'll probably do better by removing the bed knife from the mower and sharpening it on a workbench.

The reel blades can be sharpened to a limited degree with abrasive paste. Make certain first that the bed knife is properly set with minimum clearance between it and the reel. Mix 120-grit aluminum oxide or silicon-carbide powder with heavy oil or liquid dishwashing detergent to make a paste. (Valve-grinding compound can also be used.) Spread this along the upper surface of the bed knife. Then turn the reel backward by hand for a few minutes. If the spiral blades do not make light contact with the knife, scraping up the abrasive, reset the knife. You can, if you want to go to the trouble, remove the wheels, interchange the ratchet dogs and the ratchets, and replace the wheels. Pushing the mower will then turn the reel backwards for sharpening.

Abrasive sharpening should make the bed knife and reel blades noticeably keener to the touch. Rinse off all paste with water or kerosene (depending on whether the abrasive was mixed with detergent or oil) and try the mower. Some readjustment of the bed knife may be necessary for best results.

THE PRUNING SAW is basically a crosscut saw, but with extra set to the teeth for easier cutting in green wood. Sharpen it like a carpenter's crosscut saw. On a good quality pruning saw, alternate teeth are set to opposite sides, and also beveled on both the front and the trailing edges. (Economy-priced pruning saws may have teeth ground straight across, like ripsaw teeth, with-

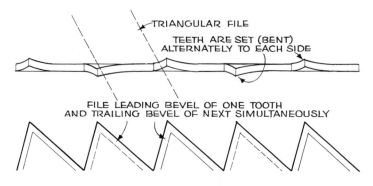

Fig. 16. Filing the teeth of a pruning saw.

out bevels. Use a magnifying glass, if necessary, to see what kind your saw has.)

Either type can usually be sharpened with a 6″ slim taper file. Clamp the saw between two wood strips in a vice, the tooth gullets only about ⅛″ above the tops of the strips to prevent file chatter. Set the file in the first gullet at one end, letting it find its own bearing against the teeth. If they are not beveled, the file will be at right angles to the blade. If the teeth have bevels, the file will be at about 65 degrees to the blade line (Figure 16).

Stand in a convenient position to file every *other* gullet, all at the same filing angle. You will be filing the leading edge of one tooth, the trailing edge of the next one. When you have filed all the alternate gullets at the same angle, change the angle to the opposite direction and file the alternate gullets you previously skipped.

Unless the saw is badly worn, four or five strokes in each gullet should serve to restore sharpness. Try to file teeth equally to avoid making some lower than the others, for on a saw all teeth should share the same work.

CHAPTER FOUR

SHARPENING COMMON HOUSEHOLD TOOLS

WHETHER they're for carving a roast or cutting out a dress, keen edges can make the difference between a hard chore and a simple task. Household tools, all too often neglected for being in the housewife's province, deserve attention because they are in such frequent use. The man who has keen saws and chisels may be shocked to discover how dull the kitchen knives are.

Fig. 1. Maximum thickness of a knife blade for cutting efficiency. When thickness reaches .002″, the knife should be sharpened.

Knife edges throw some interesting light on what makes for keenness. Skillful sharpening can give a quality knife an entering edge as thin as one *ten-thousandth* of an inch (1/10,000″, or in decimals .0001″). When use widens that edge to ten times that (1/1,000″, or .001″) the knife still cuts reasonably well. But when it's twice that thick (.002) the knife is dull and should be sharpened (Figure 1).

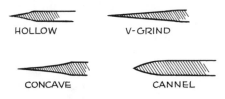

HOLLOW   V-GRIND

CONCAVE   CANNEL

Fig. 2. Four basic types of knife edges.

There are four basic kinds of knife sections, shown in Figure 2. The sturdy, flat-sided *V-grind* is commonly used on butcher knives for moderately hard use. Even stronger is the *cannel grind,* a convex section that puts plenty of metal back of the business edge. This is good for meat cleavers, which often have to stand up to bone. The popular *hollow grind,* widely used on carving knives, slips through what it cuts more easily than the V-grind. Still more so does the *concave grind,* used on knives intended for fine carving.

These shapes determine the blade bevel, but the edge bevel may be the same, or nearly the same, on all of them. An ordinary pocketknife typically has a V-grind (Figure 3), but the sides of the V do not meet to form the edge, for such a slim edge would not stand up to the duties of a pocketknife. Instead, the edge is formed by the two blade bevels. These leave more metal directly behind the edge.

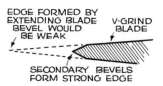

Fig. 3. V-grind on a pocketknife has secondary bevels to put more metal behind the edge.

SHARPENING WITH A STEEL. A chef's steel will keep a knife razor-sharp between grindings. Steels are tempered to a greater hardness than knife blades, and may be dead smooth (or even polished) or grooved. Grooved steels come in two types. A stripped steel has fine, straight grooves parallel to its length; a knurled steel has short, irregular grooves, also parallel to its axis. The smooth steel, often used by professional meat cutters, performs what is really a stropping operation. Grooved steels, widely used by chefs, also resharpen the blade to a degree.

Even a grooved steel removes little material, however. The main function of a steel is to reset the fine edge after it has turned up under cutting pressure. This makes the edge seem dull, but a few strokes on a steel reset the edge, and this can be done seven or eight times before more drastic sharpening in the form of grinding or whetting is required.

STONE SHARPENING is easy and effective, and can't "burn" knife edges as grinding wheels can. One type of stone resembles a steel, but being abrasive, actually removes metal to renew the edge. It may be used exactly like a steel, and the blade may be "stropped" on a steel afterwards for a fine edge. Equally good results can be had by whetting on a bench stone with one coarse and one fine side. The stone should be blocked or otherwise held so that it won't slip. Use oil or kerosene as a lubricant.

A piece of plywood with rubber-headed tacks or bits of foam plastic for feet, and a sheet of fine abrasive paper attached with rubber cement, makes a fair substitute for a stone. You can not only practice this kind of sharpening on it, but sharpen a number of knives or scissors before the abrasive paper has to be renewed.

The trailing stroke shown in the sequence of photos duplicates the action of the wet grinding wheels used by skilled cutlery makers, and gives good results. But some experts, including manufacturers of stones, advocate sliding the blade edge first against the stone as though you were peeling off a layer of

How to sharpen a carving knife with a steel. Hold the steel in your left hand (if you are right-handed) and the knife in your right, its heel under the end of the steel and the blade tilted down 15 degree (A). Then slide the knife toward you, edge first, while also moving it to the right so as to end the stroke with the blade tip near the guard of the steel (B). Now move the knife's heel to the end of the steel again, but this time with the blade on top of it and tilted up instead of down, to hone the opposite bevel (C).

it. Both methods work, so you may as well try both and find out which is easier for you.

The important thing with either method is to maintain the same bevel angle through each and every stroke, even though you flip the blade over each time. Failure to hold the same angle will prolong your efforts and form convex bevels, which aren't desirable for most purposes.

As the knife is usually longer than the stone is wide, you'll have to slide the blade sideways as you move it along the stone. For sharpening the curved tip, you can raise the handle end to bring the curved bevel into progressive contact. My own preference is to hold the blade at the same angle throughout

How to sharpen a knife on an oilstone. Hold the knife handle in your right hand, the blade tip between the thumb and forefinger of your left hand. With the handle end of the blade on the near end of the stone, cutting edge facing you, slide the knife away from you with easy pressure on the stone. Include a sideward movement so as to hone the entire length of the blade during the stroke. Finish with the blade tip on the far end of the stone. To form the best bevel, be sure to keep the angle between the blade and stone at about 15 degrees.

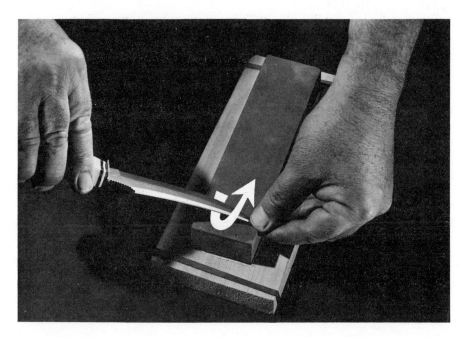

At the end of the outward stroke, flip the blade over, cutting edge away from you, and slide it back toward you, reversing the side motion so you end up at the handle end, ready to flip over and begin again. Repeat until a feather edge turns up. In hand sharpening you can't always see this, but you can feel it by sliding your finger across the flat of the blade and out past the edge. Continue until the feather edge runs the full blade length. Then take light passes over the fine side of the stone to remove the feather. As a final touch, give the edge a few strokes on a leather strop.

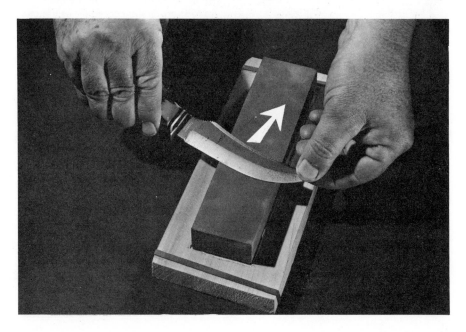

the stroke, gradually swinging the knife in a horizontal arc until most of the blade is off the stone and only the tip bevel is still on it (Figure 4).

If a knife is very dull, start on the coarse side of the stone. Remove the feather edge with a few strokes on the fine side. For a final touch, you can strop the blade on leather. You'll find this easier if you mount a short length of the strop on a board with glue or double-coated tape. Use oil with it as you would with a stone.

Pocketknives can be sharpened on small stones, preferably oiled when possible. Hold the stone by one end, near the corner of a table so that your other hand can overhang it (pocket stones are so thin you may find it difficult to hold the knife at the correct angle if your hand rests on the table). One stone manufacturer recommends an edge-first stroke, starting at the heel of the blade and ending at the tip, with the blade tilted at 25 degrees. A somewhat finer, though slightly weaker, edge is produced with a 15-degree tilt, and on a stone of this size a trailing stroke is safer so far as the stone-holding fingers are concerned.

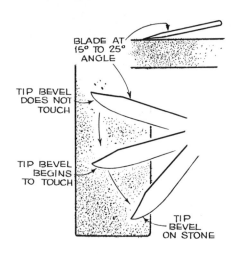

BLADE AT 15° TO 25° ANGLE

TIP BEVEL DOES NOT TOUCH

TIP BEVEL BEGINS TO TOUCH

TIP BEVEL ON STONE

Fig. 4. Method of swinging knife in an arc to sharpen the curved tip at the end of the stroke. In this case the knife is being sharpened by sliding it edge first against the stone, as opposed to the trailing stroke in the foregoing photos.

THE CUTLERY-MAKER'S METHOD. When a knife edge is nicked, it's time to grind it back far enough to establish a clean new edge. It is possible to do this on a handstone, but it is tedious. You can do it faster on a hand-turned grindstone, a power grinding head, a belt sander, or a wet grindstone. The latter is the kind used by knife makers, and they run the wheels backwards— turning away from the operator at the top. This is the reverse of usual shop practice. For ninety grinding jobs in a hundred, the wheel should turn toward you.

But knives are a special case. Their blades are long and often curved. Since you can't see the bevel being ground, you need some other means of gauging the work. The feather edge turned up as grinding proceeds can provide this. With the wheel turning away from you, grinding sparks illuminate this feather edge. Where you see it come up, that part of the blade has

Pocketknives may be sharpened dry on a small handstone, but results are better with lubrication. Slide the blade back and forth with the cutting edge trailing, keeping the angle between the blade and the stone at 15 degrees.

been thinned to keenness, while its lack shows where further grinding is necessary.

You can, however, sharpen knives on a forward-rotating wheel too. In any case, hold the blade to form a 15-degree bevel angle. On a wheel, this angle is figured from a line tangent to the wheel at the point of contact (Figure 5). A few degrees of variation won't matter, but don't change the angle once you start grinding.

In dry grinding, heat is the main problem. Knife blades are thin, and the edge temper can be drawn in an instant. Make fairly rapid passes across the wheel (or grinding belt, if you use a sander). Don't pause anywhere. Use a light touch, and either wait between passes for air to cool the blade, or dip it in water.

Reverse the knife end for end, flipping it over after each pass, to grind the opposite bevel. Watch the point of contact on the wheel. The feather edge appears as a bright silver line. Keep pressure light so that the feather will be narrow. A wide feather indicates overgrinding. In power sharpening, the

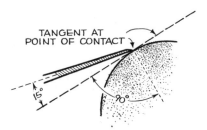

Fig. 5. Sharpening a knife on a grinding wheel. Hold blade at a 15-degree angle from a line tangent to the wheel at the point of contact. Appearance of a feather edge indicates that the blade is sufficiently ground.

feather often carries along the full length of the blade during the pass in which it first appears. A light pass with the feather edge down reduces it, and a few strokes on the fine side of an oilstone eliminate it, producing a keen edge. Leather stropping can add a final touch but isn't vital.

If most of your knives are of stainless steel, use a grinding wheel about two grades softer than those generally used for carbon steel. Popular hardware-store wheels may not bear grade designations, but mill-supply houses and dealers in machine-shop equipment offer a fuller line. The Russell Harrington Cutlery Company, maker of fine cutlery, suggests grinding stainless steel at a slower rate than carbon steel, using less pressure against the wheel and taking more time to grind every inch along the blade.

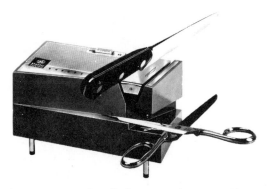

Electric sharpeners can handle knives and scissors. This one has a single wheel and two knife slots angled toward it. The blade is sharpened first against one face of the wheel, then the other. The scissors are sharpened by sliding each blade across the wheel a few times.

OTHER METHODS OF KNIFE SHARPENING. The power hone described in Chapter 2 has a wheel with coarse and fine sides, the latter usually lubricated with Vaseline. It is ideal for sharpening knives. If you use a belt sander, be sure to put on a fine-grain belt in good condition. A warped one that doesn't lie flat against the platen makes a poor sharpener.

Inexpensive little kitchen sharpeners make it easy to put a new edge on knives right where they're used. One type has a small abrasive wheel flanked by two sloping flanges, against which the knife is laid to establish the bevel angle. Another has two small fixed stones, and a third mounted on a sliding member. Slid between the stones, a knife emerges with both bevels ground to the correct angle. Other manual sharpeners have dual wheels, the inside faces sloping at the required bevel angles.

Electric sharpeners too have guides, slots, or other devices to reduce the freehand element. In these, though, too much pressure could overheat small blades. Like other kitchen sharpeners, they are meant for relatively light honing, not for grinding away damage or reconditioning blades. But they are a help in the kitchen, are easier to use than steels, and let the lady of the house have sharp knives at her service oftener than she would otherwise.

SCALLOPED CUTTING EDGES. Bread knives and other wavy-edged blades are usually beveled on one side only. Don't use a grinder or an electric sharpener. You can steel the unbeveled side. Though this won't reset the edge as well as it does straight ones, it does improve cutting action to some degree. You can also lay the unbeveled side on an oilstone and slide it along edge first, with a sideward motion as in sharpening other knives. Repeat as necessary to restore sharpness. The reason for moving the blade edge first (instead of with a trailing stroke) is that you want as little feather edge turned up as possible, because you cannot hone the beveled side to remove it.

Serrated steak knives, and others with small teeth, should be kept away from the grinding wheel or electric sharpener. By selecting a needle file that fits the serrations, you can refile them. Unworn serrations at the very tip, or near the heel, will serve as patterns for reshaping the worn ones. The gullets at the bottom of the teeth should be rounded slightly; if they are too deep or sharply angled, teeth may break off in use. As serrations are usually ground from one side of the blade only, you can use the grooves left in that side as filing guides.

To regrind scalloped or serrated knives would require special jigs similar to those used in manufacturing them. This is hardly practical for personal use. It is only fair to add that the buyer of a quality knife of this kind gets long service for his purchase dollar before the edge becomes dull enough to need attention, and if the simple methods described fail to resharpen it, a new knife will be an economical investment.

Tungsten-carbide blades, now used in some electric carving knives, are so hard they shouldn't need sharpening for a long time. Since they require special wheels, it's probably most economical to return them to the manufacturer for service. If you do try to grind such blades, a green silicon-carbide (39 Crystolon) wheel should be used.

Whatever sharpening method is used, kitchen knives should be cleaned to remove all oil, abrasive and steel dust before they are used on food.

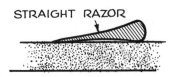

STRAIGHT RAZOR

Fig. 6. Sharpening a straight razor. Thickness of blade holds it at the correct angle when it is laid flat on the stone. Do not use a trailing stroke, but draw the blade across the stone edge first, flip it over and whet the other side.

RAZORS AND RAZOR BLADES. Regrinding is rarely necessary unless a straight razor has been outrageously abused. But whetting or honing occasionally will restore the blade to topnotch performance. The blade is hollow ground, and when it is laid flat on the stone, the thickness of the back will hold it at an angle to form a bevel of about 10 degrees on the cutting edge (Figure 6).

Holding the blade diagonally, its handle forward, draw it across the stone edge first. Use light oil or water as a lubricant. At the end of the stroke, flip the razor over, advancing the handle the other way, and push it back over the stone to whet the second bevel. Only a few strokes should be necessary. Use light pressure, but make sure the razor is flat on the stone all the time. Never use a trailing stroke. Avoid honing too much, which will turn up a fine wire edge.

Instead, finish by stropping. Be sure to hold the strop taut. If it sags under stropping pressure it will round the edge. Stropping must of course be done with a trailing stroke only. Move the razor diagonally, working from the heel to the tip; then flip the razor upside down for the next stroke. Experts make the last strokes on that side of the razor which will be next to the skin when shaving is done, so that the turned-up edge will be on the other side. Clean both the oilstone and the strop frequently with soapy water. A dirty stone can damage the edge.

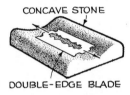

CONCAVE STONE

DOUBLE-EDGE BLADE

Fig. 7. Sharpening a double-edge razor. Use a concave stone and push the blade gently back and forth a few times, then hone the other side.

Stiff-backed, single-edge safety blades can be sharpened on a stone like a straight razor. Double-edged blades can be honed on a small concave stone made for the purpose. Don't use excessive finger pressure to press the blade against the stone, as it will bend enough to deflect the bevel contact. Stroke the blade back and forth, not arcwise (Figure 7). Flip it over to hone the opposite bevels the same way.

A stiff-backed blade can be stropped somewhat like a straight razor, the strop being laid flat. For stropping double-edged blades, try a straight (not tapering) drinking glass. Lay the blade inside and work it back and forth a few times, first one side up and then the other.

SCISSORS OF ALL KINDS. Large or small, scissors cut material by shearing it between two fairly obtuse-angled edges. At first glance the angle between the shear faces and the cutting edges (Figure 8) may seem fully 90 degrees. Actually it is about 10 degrees less. The shear faces of good scissors are hollow ground, or concave, but to such a large radius as to appear flat.

Don't sharpen scissors unless they really need it. The blades are bowed against each other so as to maintain pressure at their contact point as they open or close. Excessive grinding can reduce contact pressure until the blades no longer cut cleanly. Therefore remove as little metal as you can.

When wear is slight, as at A in Figure 9, there will be a narrow bright line along the top of the shear face. Sharpness can be restored by whetting the edge back to the dotted line, when the wear line on the shear face will vanish. But excessive wear as at B will show a wider band on the face. Edge sharpening would require grinding back much farther, while grinding the shear faces to the dotted arc isn't practical without special equipment.*

Sharpening for only moderate wear can be done by hand on a stone, or on a belt sander or a grinding wheel. The abrasive should be fine grained, and moved across the edge only, not along it. The reason for this is that the serrations so left in the edges will hold material being cut. Without such serrations, it tends to skid toward the blade tips.

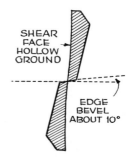

Fig. 8. Scissors in cross section. Shear face may look flat but is actually hollow ground; edges are beveled about 10 degrees.

For wheel or belt sharpening, carefully set the tool rest or table to the desired bevel angle, taking into account any slope on the back of the blade (Figure 10). Wheel or belt travel should be into the edge, not trailing. Open the scissors wide and place one blade, shear face up, on the tool rest or table. Bring the edge into light contact with the abrasive and immediately draw the blade across from right to left at a uniform rate of speed so that grinding is even all along the edge. Don't stop anywhere. Make another pass or two until the narrow flat on the shear face disappears, but no more. Then turn the shears upside down to grind the edge of the other blade the same way.

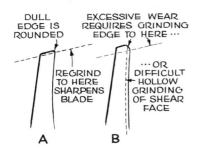

Fig. 9. Slightly dull scissors blades (A) need to be ground only enough to get rid of rounded edge. When blades are excessively worn (B), the edges must be ground farther back, or the shear faces must be hollow ground.

Closing the scissors will remove the small burr left by grinding. Any feather edge left on the outside face of the blades should be removed with a fine-cut file or a small stone. If left on, this feather edge will catch and pull threads.

* Grinding shear faces calls for a big wheel, from 26″ to 32″ in diameter. One way to approximate this curvature in the home shop may be with a shoe of appropriate radius clamped under a sanding belt. It could be made of hardwood, sanded smooth and waxed to minimize belt friction. A maker of sharpening equipment, Norton Company, Worcester, MA 01606, offers formed abrasive disks with radiuses equal to those of the large wheels mentioned. These will hone the shear faces of scissors properly if used with a jig or other device to insure uniform action.

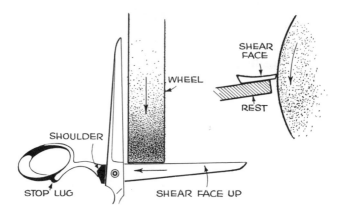

Fig. 10. Sharpening scissors on a grinding wheel. The tool rest should be set at the required bevel angle, and the wheel should travel toward the edge.

For hand whetting, place a bench stone near the right-hand edge of a bench or table. Opening the scissors wide, hold the upper blade diagonally on the stone at the correct bevel angle. The shear face of the blade being whetted will be facing you. Draw the scissors toward you while moving it gradually to the right to whet the entire length of the blade at each stroke. Turn the scissors around to whet the other blade in the same way.

Some knife sharpeners, including the newer electric ones, have an extra slot that will hold scissors blades at the correct angle. They'll sharpen any but left-handed shears, on which they would grind the bevel angle backwards. Unless you have a still newer sharpener with a special slot for left-handed scissors, this kind will have to be custom sharpened as described above, with due care to get the bevels right.

Scissors blades are sharpened on a bench stone with the shear face up and moved edge first across the stone at the proper bevel angle. After several strokes, turn the scissors over and whet the other blade.

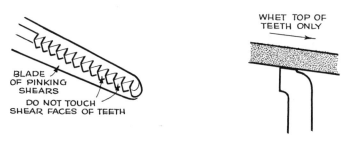

Fig. 11. Sharpen pinking shears by whetting only the tops of the teeth.

Pinking shears are relatively expensive. The safest thing to do when they're dull is to send them to the manufacturer for resharpening. Should you try to do it yourself, don't touch the shear faces (the notches between the teeth). Grind or whet only the top edge of the teeth, which corresponds to the edges of ordinary shears (Figure 11).

If you use a wheel or belt, take great care not to overgrind. It's safer to clamp one blade in a vise, edge up, and use a handstone to whet the top edge, stroking the stone across it from the toothed side to the back of the blade. (A scissors sharpener, made by Blackhawk Supply Company of Sheldahl, Iowa, and shown in a photo, makes this action foolproof and automatic.) Clean off oil and whetting dust before closing the blades.

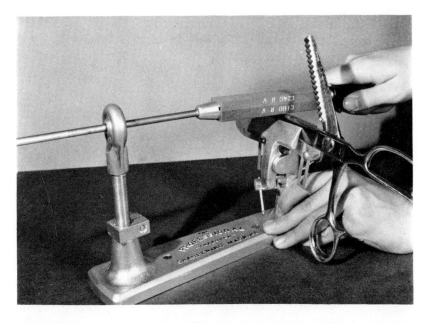

Sharpening device made by Blackhawk Supply, Sheldahl, Iowa 50243, simplifies the job of whetting pinking shears, other shears, and scissors. Here a blade of a pair of pinking shears is being whetted across the top.

After sharpening scissors blades, check the pivot action. If the blades are too loose the contact point between them may be opening, so that material falls between the blades instead of being cut. Try tightening the pivot screw slightly. If this doesn't pull the blades closer together, the screw head may be excessively worn. Get a new screw if you can. If this isn't possible, the old screw can sometimes be spread by striking a center punch set in the middle of the slot. Test the pivot action after each blow to avoid getting the blades too tight.

Some pivots are simple rivets, and can be tightened with a few hammer blows. But take care not to tighten the pivot if it doesn't need it. It may be downright loose with the blades wide open, for example, only to tighten up as soon as the blades are partly closed. In such a case, don't tighten the pivot. Be sure to check action frequently if you do, for it's difficult to reverse the process. Blades that are set too tight will quickly become dull from cutting into each other.

After repeated grindings, the blade tips may no longer meet (Figure 12). One way to remedy this is to grind a little off the lug on one eye that acts as a stop when the scissors are closed (see Figure 10). It may also be necessary to grind a little clearance between the shoulders. With forged blades, it is possible instead to hold one blade on the edge of a vise and with a few light blows of a hammer bend the handle end out slightly to let the blade close farther. But cast-steel blades will surely break if this is attempted.

Your fingers are a fairly good judge of whether a scissors is sharp. Drawn gently across (never along) an edge, they can at once tell you whether it's sharp or only nearly so. Scissors can be tested on thin silk, wet newspaper, or facial tissue. It takes a really keen blade to slit facial tissue cleanly instead of ruffling it up.

Fig. 12. Blade tips of scissors may not meet after repeated grindings. Grinding down the lug on one eye will remedy this.

HOME HAIR CLIPPERS will pull painfully when they're dull. Unscrew the pivot nut to take them apart, taking note of the spring or washer so that you can assemble it precisely the same way. Separate the blades, spread fine valve-grinding compound evenly on the inside surfaces of both, and with one blade flat on the table place the other on top, the abrasive-coated surfaces together. Now move the top blade in a circular motion with moderate pressure, lifting if from time to time. Add abrasive compound and a little oil occasionally.

This honing action should take place over both the cutting surfaces near the teeth, and the sliding surfaces at the back of the blades. If you find it awkward to maintain full contact in the manner described, you can instead hone each blade separately on a piece of plate glass or a flat-machined piece of iron or steel. Spread the grinding compound on thinly, with a little oil, and rub both blades of the clippers on it, inside surfaces down, with a circular motion.

When the honed surfaces show a uniform dull sheen all over, including those areas on the teeth, clean off all grinding compound meticulously with kerosene, lighter fluid, or a similar solvent. Take care to get it out from between the teeth. Reassemble the clippers with a little light oil on the sliding surfaces.

CHAPTER FIVE

SHARPENING ALL KINDS OF SAWS

A POWER saw is only as good as its blade. A dull blade may chew its way through lumber, but you won't like the job. It will leave rough or burned edges, feed hard, wander off the line. At the end of a long extension cord, it can blow fuse after fuse.

Sure, you can get circular saws resharpened at moderate cost. But being able to do it yourself may make the difference between finishing a weekend job or not. Also, once friends and neighbors know that you can put a new bite on saw blades, you may have a spare-time business.

Except for carbide-tipped blades, which require grinding, all blades can be resharpened with files. Other needed equipment is so simple you can make it yourself. Often a little touch-up filing of the right sort will make a blade cut like new again. But if a blade has been hard used, or sharpened so often that the teeth have become short or have lost their set, it must be reconditioned by the following steps:

Jointing, which means bringing all the teeth to precisely the same height. Any low ones won't do their share of the work. Jointing can be done by grinding, stoning, or filing. As evidence that no low teeth remain, all of them should show a tiny flat area at their tip, instead of a point.

Shaping, ideally, restores teeth to their original size and contour. It's necessary only when hard use or repeated jointing or filing has left the teeth too small or misshapen to cut well.

Gumming deepens the rounded gullets between teeth to bring the teeth back to full depth. It's done on a round-edge abrasive wheel or with a round file.

Setting restores the alternate right- and left-hand bends at the tips of the teeth. This "set" makes the teeth cut a kerf wider than the thickness of the blade, and is essential to free cutting, except in the case of hollow-ground blades. You can tell when a blade needs setting by the narrowness of the kerf it cuts, and often by the binding of the blade body in the kerf. On a handsaw, you can compare the set of most of the teeth with those near or under the handle. As these get almost no use, they usually retain their original set after hard-worked teeth have lost theirs.

Filing, the final step, restores the bevels and edges of reshaped teeth. Sometimes light filing is all that is needed to sharpen a saw that is otherwise in good condition. In other words, it may be the first and only step, or the final one in the sequence given.

As a guide to resharpening, it's wise to make a pattern of each new blade you buy, especially circular saws, in which all the teeth wear simultaneously, leaving no unused ones as a guide in reconditioning. Trace around a number of teeth with a very sharp pencil. Make notes about bevel angles and the amount and depth of tooth set.

The first step in reconditioning any blade is to remove pitch and gum with lacquer thinner, benzine, acetone, or a solvent sold for the purpose. Take the time to get off all deposits. Any traces left on will impede sharpening.

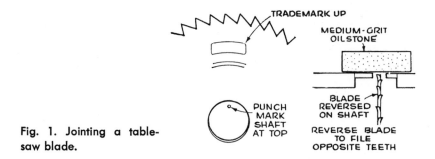

Fig. 1. Jointing a table-saw blade.

Jointing a table-saw blade. Mount it on its arbor with the teeth pointing backwards. Have the trademark up as you tighten the nut. If the arbor is bent, make a punch mark on top at its end (Figure 1). Provided the blade is now jointed, and always replaced with the punch mark and trademark up, it will run true despite a bent arbor or slightly oversize hole.

With the blade running, carefully raise it (or lower the table) until the teeth just barely graze an oilstone held flat on the table. A large flat file may be used too, though it may have to be blocked up off the table. Take great care to avoid letting the saw teeth bite in suddenly or fling the stone or file off the table.

Very, very slowly feed the blade up (or the table down) $\frac{1}{64}$". Stop the saw often to inspect results, and move the stone or file occasionally to work against a new area. (Don't use a costly Arkansas or other good stone.) Joint only until all the teeth show a small shiny area on their tips.

The same jointing procedure generally applies to a radial-arm saw. It will be necessary, however, to block the stone by putting a piece of wood behind it. Then carefully lower the running blade until it barely touches the stone.

The chisel-edged raker teeth on combination blades are a special case. They should be $\frac{1}{64}$" to $\frac{1}{32}$" shorter than the crosscut teeth. Therefore they may show no jointing marks. They should be jointed separately, as shown in the accompanying photo.

Circular-saw teeth can also be jointed by filing. To insure getting them all the same length, either a homemade or a commercial jig is required. Either must provide a well-fitting arbor for the blade, and a positive stop for the filing action.

To joint raker teeth on a table-saw arbor, adjust the blade height so the blade can be locked by clamping down a piece of plywood pressed into a raker gullet, with the back of the next raker parallel to the table. Block up a mill file to joint this raker $\frac{1}{32}''$ shorter than crosscut teeth. Index to the next raker by shifting the stop to the following gullet. The same setup can be used for filing top bevels on other teeth by tilting the arbor. For opposite angle on alternate teeth, you simply mount the blade backwards.

Shaping circular-saw teeth. Mark the new bottoms of regular and raker teeth by holding a pencil against the blade while turning it *by hand* on the arbor. With the blade in a wooden clamp (Figure 2), shape the teeth to their original form and size by filing.

File straight across, but only until the flats left by jointing just disappear, and the gullets touch the scribed circles. Use a triangular file to shape crosscut teeth, a mill file with a rounded or ground-off edge for other teeth, and a round file for gullets. File on the push stroke only, lifting the file on the return stroke. Take care not to file nicks, for these readily become the starts of cracks, once stressed in use.

Setting circular-saw teeth. Hollow-ground blades, which taper thinner inwards from the rim, require no tooth set. On other blades, set all but the raker teeth found on combination saws. Setting is always necessary after shaping, but may not be required every time a saw is sharpened.

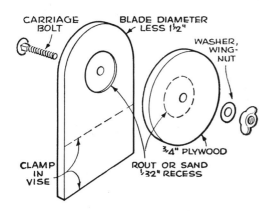

Fig. 2. Homemade vise for shaping circular-saw blades. Cut out facing center recesses to provide a firm grip on the blade near the tooth line. With the blade clamped firmly in the vise, shape the teeth to their original form and size by filing.

You can buy circular-saw setters for mounting on the workbench or in a slot of your table saw. A homemade one is shown in Figure 3. The anvil is a $\frac{3}{8}$" machine bolt with one side of the head filed to a 10-degree bevel. The distance the teeth overhang the anvil determines the set and must be carefully adjusted by moving the plywood slide which is held by screws in chamfered slots. When the blade is in the right position, tighten the screws to hold the slide firmly in place. Turn each tooth into position on the anvil by revolving the blade on the dowel, and set it with a square-tipped punch and a hammer by bending the tooth over the anvil. Take care to set the teeth in the same direction they were originally; reversing the set may break them. Set every other tooth; then turn the blade over to set the alternate ones. On wide-topped teeth, set only the sharp tips at the front, not the entire tooth.

Bend only the tips of the teeth, and never to more than one-third their depth. Recommended depth is $\frac{1}{16}$" of the tooth tip on fine-toothed crosscut

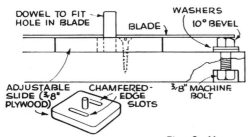

Fig. 3. Homemade saw setter.

and plywood saws, $\frac{3}{32}''$ for rip, combination, and nail-cutter blades. The amount each tooth is set over varies from one-fourth to one-third its thickness, the lesser set for small-toothed blades or those meant for very smooth cuts, such as cabinet combination blades; the one-third set for rip, nail-cutter, and chisel-tooth and combination blades to be used on electric handsaws. (For use on table saws, combination blades should be set one-fourth tooth thickness.)

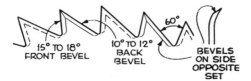

Fig. 4. Crosscut saw.

File-sharpening the teeth. Clamp the blade in a saw vise. (Never put it in a common vise, which may permanently damage the blade.) Use a round-edge mill file for rip and chisel teeth, a slim-taper triangular file for crosscut and combination-blade teeth.

On chromium-surfaced blades, use a firm stroke and ample pressure to get through the hard surface. Start with one or two rocking strokes. Remove as little metal as possible.

For crosscut teeth, file the face of one and the back of the next separately. Remember that the filed bevels should always be on the side of the tooth away from the direction it is set, as in Figure 4. (Though teeth on hollow-ground blades aren't set, they, too, are beveled on opposite sides.) File only until the bevel touches the far corner of the chisel tip left by shaping. After filing alternate teeth, turn the blade around to file the others.

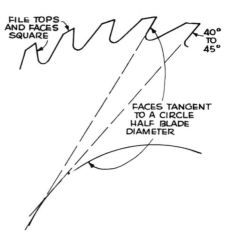

Fig. 5. Ripsaw.

File ripsaw teeth straight across at 90 degrees (Figure 5), but file alternate teeth from one side, and those between from the other side, to equalize filing stresses and burrs. Be careful not to nick the gullets. If reshaping is not necessary, sharpen by filing only the tops of ripsaw teeth straight across, until the flats left by jointing just disappear (Figure 5).

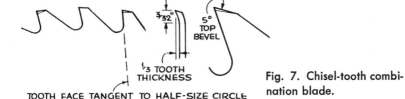

Fig. 6. Combination blade.

RAKERS ⅟32" LOW

CROSSCUT TEETH
SET AND BEVELED
ALTERNATELY

Combination blades may have two kinds of teeth, or only one. The raker teeth in the first type are filed straight across (Figure 6), while the crosscut teeth are alternately beveled.

Chisel-tooth utility or combination blades (Figure 7) are filed straight across on the tooth faces. But a 5-degree bevel, alternately left and right, is filed on the back of each tooth. For touch-up sharpening, file the top bevels only. Use more top bevel for softwoods, less for hard.

³⁄32"

5° TOP BEVEL

⅓ TOOTH THICKNESS

TOOTH FACE TANGENT TO HALF-SIZE CIRCLE

Fig. 7. Chisel-tooth combination blade.

Nail-cutter blades, though of special alloy steel, can also be filed. File the tooth faces straight (90 degrees). The back bevel is critical. Be sure to duplicate the original tooth shape (Figure 8).

DUPLICATE ORIGINAL BACK ANGLE AND BEVEL

SET ³⁄32" DEEP, ⅓ TOOTH THICKNESS

Fig. 8. Nail-cutter blade.

Cabinet combination blades have wide-topped teeth that should be filed at 90 degrees, both on the faces and tops. File every other tooth, then reverse the blade to file intervening ones (Figure 9).

Thin plywood blades are filed straight across, with no bevels. Take care not to overfile the small crosscut teeth.

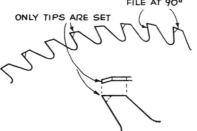

FILE AT 90°

ONLY TIPS ARE SET

Fig. 9. Cabinet combination blade.

Sharpening dado heads. For jointing, mount the outside cutters alone on the arbor with the teeth backwards, staggering them so that the blades will lie flat against each other despite the set of the crosscut teeth. When all these show jointing flats, joint each raker tooth separately $\frac{1}{64}''$ shorter. Mount the inside cutters (chippers) separately. Joint these also $\frac{1}{64}''$ short.

JOINT
RAKERS
$\frac{1}{64}''$ SHORT

SPURS IN EACH GROUP
SET AND BEVELED ALIKE

Fig. 10. Dado blade, crosscut teeth.

All spurs (crosscut teeth) of a group in the outside blades are set and beveled in the same direction, those in the next group in the other (Figure 10). Rakers are filed square and not set. Figure 11 shows another type of outside blade having two big oppositely set crosscut teeth and an unset raker in each group.

SET AND
BEVEL
TWO
TEETH
OPPOSITELY

FILE
RAKER
AT 90°

Fig. 11. Dado blade, raker teeth.

FILE TOPS OF CHIPPERS
STRAIGHT ACROSS

Sharpen chippers by filing only the tops square across, and only until the jointing flats just disappear.

Resharpening bandsaw blades. This can pay if you have a job that must be done and only a dull blade on hand. Hold the blade between boards in a vise, as in Figure 12, or mount it inside out on the bandsaw (teeth facing up for filing), between clamped blocks.

Tooth set should be proportionate to blade width and tooth depth, and parallel to the blade back as shown, not angled. More set promotes free cutting on curves, less makes for better straight tracking. An ordinary hand set, or a homemade one on the order of Figure 3, but with a straight blade-alignment strip, may be used.

File teeth after setting to restore the 90-degree chisel tips. Use a slim-taper triangular file that will leave a small radius in the gullets. The hook of the teeth is produced by tilting the file. Use the same number of strokes on each tooth.

It's best to file the teeth set toward you first, and reverse the blade to file the others. This leaves the filing burr inside, and the blade is more likely to track true than if filed from one side only. After filing, equalize the tooth set by touching an oilstone lightly to each side of the running blade.

Saber-saw blades. These are worth resharpening only if no replacement is at hand. File the tooth faces at about 8 degrees right and left, or to their original shape and bevel. There is usually an unused tooth or two at the chuck end for comparison.

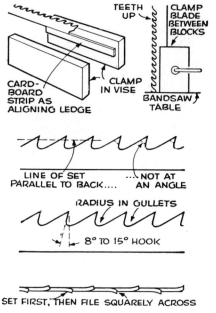

Fig. 12. Bandsaw blade.

RECONDITIONING HANDSAWS. Don't even try to sharpen these fine-toothed saws unless you are prepared to give them the time and attention the job requires. For your first attempt, it's a good idea to practice on an old saw. A good light and even a magnifying glass may be necessary. If you want to sharpen handsaws with a minimum of practice and effort, it may pay to consider some of the commercial helps mentioned farther on in this chapter. Though not foolproof, they can minimize the chances of error and enable you to do a fairly good job the first time.

Use wood strips if you have to hold a handsaw in an ordinary vise. A saw vise is better in that it eliminates fumbling with strips, but may not be worth buying for only an occasional job. Clamp the blade close to the tooth line to prevent chattering.

Joint the teeth first, if they are of uneven height, either with a commercial jointer or with a flat file clamped to a wood block as shown in the accompanying photo. Don't overdo it; joint only until a minute flat appears on *every* tooth. Jointing too much will commit you to more work in reshaping.

If shaping is necessary, file squarely across one gullet (with a triangular file) until the jointing flats on both sides are half their size. Skip a gullet and do the same. Then reverse the saw to file in the skipped gullets, which should

To joint the teeth of a handsaw, clamp a mill file to a squared wood block with the file edge projecting. Use the block as a guide as you push the file along the tops of the teeth. Stop when each tooth shows a shiny spot. You can also use a commerical saw jointer if you have one.

make the halved jointing flats disappear altogether. File only until they do. Filing from both sides equalizes steel stresses and is preferable to doing all the work from one side of the blade.

Compare used and unused teeth (those nearest the handle). This will show whether setting is necessary, and how much set the teeth should be given. A handsaw set assures uniformity and is adjustable. The set should never be more than half a tooth's length or half a tooth's thickness. Taper and hollow-ground handsaws are set much less than this.

Adjust the hand set and use it to set every other tooth. Then reverse the saw in the vise to set the others. Be sure you set teeth in the same direction as they were originally, and all alike. Never reverse the set. It's a good idea to joint again lightly after shaping and setting, both to insure equal tooth height and as a guide to filing.

An inexpensive filing guide, such as the one here made by A.D. McBurney, is handy to have in your workshop. It will keep your file at the proper bevel angle, allowing you to concentrate on filing in the right gullets and cutting them to the proper depth.

To file crosscut teeth, clamp the saw with its handle to your right at first. Standing at the left, lay a fine triangular file in front of the first tooth set *toward* you, as in Figure 13, angling the file with its handle to your left so that it will form the front bevel of this tooth and the back bevel of the one ahead of it at the same time. Hold the file level or with its handle a bit high, but never down.

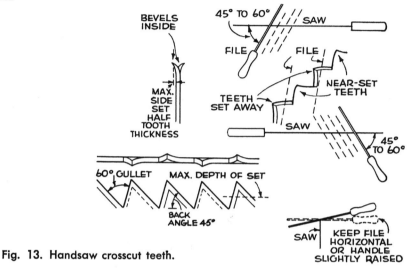

Fig. 13. Handsaw crosscut teeth.

File until jointing marks are halved, skip one tooth to file the front of the next one set toward you, and so on. When all the near-set teeth have been filed, reverse the saw in the vise, its handle to the left. Stand at the right and again file the front of those teeth set toward you, until the jointing marks disappear entirely.

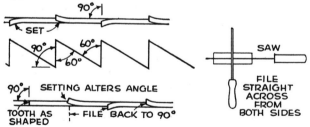

Fig. 14. Ripsaw teeth.

Ripsaw teeth are simpler, being unbeveled, but setting will make the tooth fronts something less than 90 degrees in the direction *across* the blade. Restore them to this by filing directly across (Figure 14). But file every other tooth from one side of the blade, then reverse the saw to file those in between.

One more step adds a final touch to a good job of saw sharpening. Lay the handsaw flat and rub a *fine* stone just *once*—and very lightly—along the sides of the teeth on both sides of the blade. This corrects minor inaccuracies in jointing and removes filing burr. Should a saw run to one side in cutting—

that is, persistently tend to saw away from the line—stone the teeth this way once more on that side.

Utility and keyhole saws usually resemble ripsaws, having tooth fronts at 90 degrees to the tooth line instead of sloping like crosscut teeth, and teeth that are set but not beveled. They are resharpened like ripsaw teeth. Some miter saws have teeth shaped like crosscut teeth, but smaller, with less set, and not beveled. Their size makes them difficult to sharpen, though it's possible with a fine file and a magnifying glass.

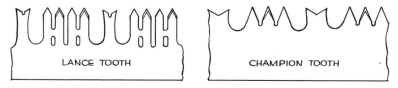

LANCE TOOTH   CHAMPION TOOTH

Fig. 15. Two types of timber saw.

Pruning and timber saws, like certain combination circular saws, have two kinds of teeth set in groups. The crosscut teeth are set and beveled alternately on opposite sides. The raker teeth, which clear out chips left by the cutters, are neither set nor beveled, but have edges on both sides so that they clear the kerf whether pushed or pulled. Figure 15 shows two styles.

Joint all the teeth if any are short, using a file clamped to a block or a commercial jointer tool. Then joint the raker teeth separately so that their tops are from 1/100″ to 1/64″ below the tops of the cutter teeth. Be sure you make them all the same height. Reshape worn teeth if necessary by copying less used ones at the end of the blade, using a round file or a round-edged mill file to deepen the gullets. These must be well rounded, and the "V" in raker teeth symmetrical. If there are small round gullets between crosscut teeth, use a small round file to dress or deepen them, should reshaping require it.

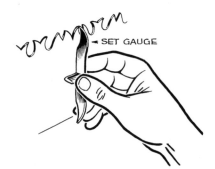

◄ SET GAUGE

Fig. 16. Setting gauge checks uniformity of teeth as work proceeds. Set only crosscut teeth.

Leave raker teeth unset. Set crosscut teeth to a depth no more than a third of their height, and to an amount no more than half their thickness—or even less for sawing hardwoods. Remember to set teeth only in their original direction of set, and all equally. A setting gauge (Figure 16) will check this, though a good setter almost automatically assures it.

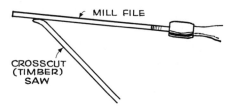

Fig. 17. When filing cutter teeth of crosscut timber saw, clamp the blade at a 45-degree angle, leaning away from you. This makes it easier to file the teeth at the proper angle.

For filing the cutter teeth, try to clamp the blade at a 45-degree angle, leaning away from you, as in Figure 17. You'll be able to reach the teeth more readily and file them at the proper angle more comfortably in this position. Use a triangular saw file or a mill file of appropriate size to bevel and sharpen the crosscut teeth. Again, file alternate teeth from one side of the blade and then reverse it to file the others. The bevels are of course toward you as you file, and always on the inside of the set. Some sharpeners recommend a round-edge mill file, which will deepen a gullet while filing the outer bevel on the first crosscut tooth at the same time.

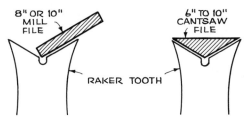

Fig. 18. Filing raker teeth with a mill file or a cantsaw file.

Reclamp the blade in a vertical position to file the raker teeth. A square-edged mill file may be used to file each of the inside edges straight across as in Figure 18. A cantsaw file will do both edges at once, as shown in the same drawing. Hold either file perfectly level, and file straight across, leaving the points of the tooth sharp.

Bucksaws are sharpened like hand crosscut saws, preferably with the blade removed from the frame and clamped between boards or in a saw vise. But they can be sharpened in their frames. Place one end of the frame on a low support with the top of the frame near you and the blade away. Holding the blade in the area you're filing, file both sides of every tooth set away from you, bringing it to a sharp point. Turn the frame over to present the other side of the blade for filing the remaining teeth.

SAW-SHARPENING AIDS. Because saw sharpening is something of a precision job, special jigs or accessories can go far toward producing good results. A hand set is worth having if you frequently sharpen handsaws. For circular

This setter takes circular-saw blades to 10″ diameter, sets each tooth alike with a blow on the punch while your other hand remains free to turn the blade from tooth to tooth.

saws, there is a setter that fits into a groove of the table saw, and another that can be used on top of a workbench. A hammer tap or two on one of these sets each tooth accurately.

For jointing circular saws by hand, there is an accessory that provides an arbor mount to insure concentricity and a guide that limits filing depth. Together these enable one to joint all teeth accurately to equal length. The same manufacturer offers a device for both jointing and sharpening. It has two rollers to limit filing depth, an indexer to lock teeth successively in filing position, and a slide that guides the file at the proper angle.

If you have a jigsaw, the wooden jig shown in a photo and in Figure 19 will enable you to sharpen circular saws quite well. The outer jig frame is clamped to the jigsaw table, its cleat abutting the table front. The slide has a bolt threaded horizontally into its end; the bolt hits the inside of the U-shaped frame to serve as a stop so that each tooth will be filed to the same degree. A plain dowel or a headless screw will serve as an index pin if you lift the blade to move to the next tooth. The pivoted stop is an alternative. It's a little handier, as the blade need only be turned to let the dog drop into the next tooth, and then backed slightly as far as the stop pin permits.

The blade arbor must be a close fit in the arbor hole. A piece of hardwood dowel, steel shafting, pipe, or metal tubing may be used. The photo shows the blade tilted up by a block for filing a 5-degree bevel on the tops of combination-blade teeth. For filing the bevels of crosscut teeth, the jigsaw table is tilted instead. A file made for jigsaw use is best, but you can break an ordinary taper file to suitable length and grind its tang to fit the blade chuck.

Grinding circular saws produces superior results if accurately done. But this requires a fixture for holding the blade and presenting it to the wheel at the proper angle, along with some means of indexing each tooth in turn. Two low-priced saw-grinding accessories make use of the table or bench saw as a grinding head, the wheel being mounted on the saw arbor. The blade is mounted on a fixture that slides in a table slot. One such unit will sharpen blades up to 10″ diameter. Another will accommodate blades up to 12″. Still larger saw-grinding machines are available for those wishing to go into the business of saw sharpening.

A saw vise and filing guide are combined in this tool. A quick-acting clamp locks the blade with one tooth in filing position. File slides on a ramp that controls both bevel and cross angles, and on rollers that limit filing depth. The unit can be used for jointing, too. Its maker also sells a less-expensive device that is used for jointing only.

Mount a grinding wheel on your table-saw arbor, and with this Sears accessory you can joint, shape, or sharpen circular-saw blades up to 12″ diameter. The device is adjustable for bevel angles and indexes the teeth. With a suitable wheel, even carbide-tipped blades can be sharpened.

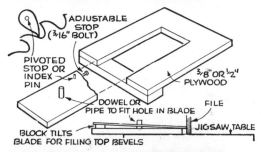

Fig. 19. You can use a jigsaw to speed shaping and filing of circular-saw blades by fitting it with the jig shown. The wooden slide must be a close fit; its stop is a bolt threaded directly into an undersized hole on the wood. The index pin may be a stub of dowel, or a hardwood tooth pivoted on a screw. Crosscut teeth are beveled by tilting the jigsaw table. To file a top bevel on other teeth, tilt the blade up with a block (arrow) placed under it opposite the file. A file made for use in the jigsaw is best, though an old one may be broken to size and ground to fit the machine's chuck.

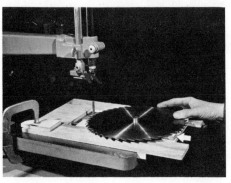

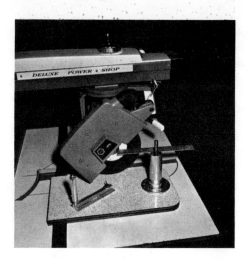

On a radial saw, you can completely recondition small or large circular saws up to 24" in diameter. Fasten a plywood auxiliary table to a strip that can be clamped in place of the usual fence strip. On the auxiliary table fasten a blade mount (1½" pipe in a floor flange) with a ½" rod centered in it. The rod can be pinned in, or threaded and screwed into an undersize hole in the table. In use, the blade (represented by a steel rule above) should be slightly below grinding-wheel center. An adjustable edge support (left of wheel) may be made of wood or metal. This one has a ball-bearing caster on top for easy blade movement.

The blade is centered and held down by a steel cone locked on the shaft with a setscrew. The edge support is set just inside the tooth line. Blades can be jointed, gummed and sharpened. Here one is being gummed (reshaped). The wheel is pulled straight in along the front of each tooth, and the blade turned slightly to round the gullet. The setup is then altered to grind along the sloping backs of the teeth. The magnetic pointer shown indicates the tooth at which grinding was begun. The wheel guard, here raised to show the operation better, should be kept as low as practicable.

Grinding crosscut teeth at an angle is done like this, with the motor carriage tilted. To grind alternate teeth, the carriage is tilted to the opposite angle and if necessary readjusted as to height. Tops of chisel-type teeth can also be ground by raising or lowering the wheel to form the desired angle. The blade-retaining cone can be purchased ready-made.

Forward travel of the motor carriage and grinding wheel is positively controlled by an adjustable stop—a C-clamp locked inside one of the carriage ways, as shown above. A short ½" rod pinned or welded to the clamp lies in the V-way. The clamp body is tapped for a bolt, which stops carriage movement and provides a fine adjustment.

SHARPENING CHAIN SAWS. There are three main types of chain saws, the most common—and easiest to sharpen—being the round-hooded or chipper chain. Figure 20 shows the elements making up this kind. Right and left-hand cutters are mounted on both sides of the drive links that engage the sprocket, with plain tie straps between the cutters.

These round-hooded cutters are sharpened with a round file, so held that its radius forms a like undercut at the top of the tooth. The angle of this undercut is critical. If it has too much rake or hook, the chain will grab and dull rapidly. If it has too little rake, or none, the chain will cut slowly, require more cutting pressure, or tend to rise from the kerf.

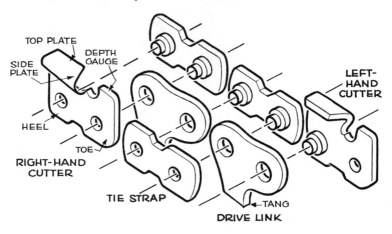

Fig. 20. Most common type of chain saw consists of round-hooded cutters mounted on both sides of drive links.

If possible, remove the chain for sharpening. The work is best done in a suitable vise that holds the chain at waist height. If you are right handed, mount the vise so that you can work from its front and its right-hand end as in Figure 21. You can then file left-hand cutters while standing at the end of the vise (the chain always being clamped in with its cutting edges pointing away from you). You would file right-hand cutters while standing in front of the vise.

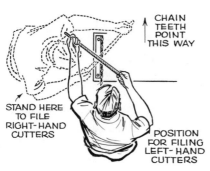

Fig. 21. Correct positions for filing the cutters of a chain saw.

Fig. 22. Proper file for sharpening cutters on McCulloch saws will extend ⅐ of its diameter above top of tooth; ⅒ for cutters on Oregon saws.

If you are left-handed, the vise should be mounted to let you file the right-hand cutters while standing at the left-hand end, and left-hand cutters while standing in front of the vise. In all cases you should be filing from inside to the outside of a tooth. This leads filings away from the links.

If you have to file the saw chain on the machine, tighten chain tension enough to keep the links rigid under filing pressure. If possible, cut into a stump to half the depth of the chain bar, and let the saw stand in this kerf. You will thus have both hands free for filing.

It's a good idea to have a new cutter of the type used in your chain on hand to compare with the results of your filing. You will also need a round chain-saw file of the right size. Check your saw manual and the manufacturer's chain designation to make sure, for the size of the file automatically governs the undercut angle and can make or break the sharpening job. The proper file for McCulloch chains will, when in filing position, extend a distance of one-seventh its diameter above the top of the tooth. But on Oregon saw chains only one-tenth of the file should lie above the tooth (Figure 22). Other chains may vary from these.

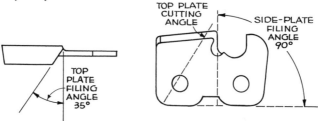

Fig. 23. Proper filing should sharpen the top plates and side plates simultaneously at the angles shown.

Hold the file level and at an angle of 35 degrees across the chain (that is, at 55 degrees to the length of the chain) as in Figure 23. File on the forward stroke only, pressing the file into the tooth and away from the gullet. Use long, slow strokes. File all the teeth to the same length (one way to do this is to count equal strokes). You must, however, file away all of the dulled edge, or the saw will remain cutting-sharp only for a short time.

Be careful not to rock the file up or down, but hold it level for the full length of every stroke. Lift the file out of contact on each back stroke; to let it drag will only dull its teeth. Rotate the file on each back stroke to equalize wear all around its circumference.

Correct filing (and the proper file) should simultaneously form the 35-degree top plate and 90-degree side plate angles shown in Figure 23. Compare the result of filing with a new cutter, if you have one.

File all the teeth on one side first. Then proceed to file the other set. Don't file right- and left-hand cutters alternately; the experts say you'll never do a good job that way. Be sure you use the same 35-degree filing angle on both sets of teeth. If those on one side are sharpened to a more acute angle, the saw will pull persistently to that side.

Saw-chain makers offer filing guides that will help you maintain the correct filing angle. They also provide a comfortable grip on the file. Follow the instructions provided with them.

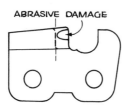

ABRASIVE DAMAGE

Fig. 24. If cutters have been damaged, it is necessary to file away the damaged part—for example, to the dotted line in this drawing.

A saw that has been operated in mud or sand, or that has hit rock, may show abrasive damage as in Figure 24. File away all the damaged part of the teeth, back to the dotted line in the drawing. Any chain saw operated under abrasive conditions will of course have to be sharpened often.

When teeth have been filed halfway back, they sometimes tend to bind in the kerf. Some manufacturers recommend filing such teeth at a 45-degree angle instead of 35. Check your saw manual first, however.

Set depth gauges too. That part of each cutter just forward of the gullet is called the depth gauge, for it determines how far into the wood the cutter can sink at a single pass. Because the top plate slopes backwards, filing the cutting edge necessarily lowers the tooth slightly. Therefore the depth gauge too must be filed lower to maintain the necessary depth of cut.

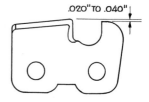

.020" TO .040"

Fig. 25. Depth gauges must be filed lower to correspond with the slightly lowered cutting edges. A depth-gauge tool insures lowering all the depth gauges equally.

This is done with a fine flat file, held perfectly level and at 90 degrees to the chain. To insure lowering all the depth gauges equally, it's wise to use a depth-gauge tool. This is a steel stamping, stepped at the ends, which is laid on top of the cutters. Filing across the stepped ends, which are slotted to let the depth gauge protrude, quickly sets all of them to uniform depth. Some depth-gauge tools have four stepped ends for as many settings.

For saws with direct drive, or low power, the depth gauges should be only .020″ to .030″ below the teeth. For average-power saws they may be set as low as .035″, and for powerful or geared saws up to .040″ (Figure 25). Still lower settings may be used for soft woods, while for hard or frozen woods the settings given may be too great. The right setting is the one that lets the chain cut freely.

After filing them to depth, the depth gauges should be smoothly rounded off in front. This is done by filing straight across with a flat file, but tilting it a bit sideways at each stroke to form a well-rounded profile. Don't file a slant instead; it will cut a furrow and hamper tooth action. Leave about half of the top of the depth gauge flat, and in no case less than one and a half times its width.

Chisel and crosscut saw chains require expert filing and are more difficult to sharpen. Get specific instructions for these, and follow them carefully.

Inspect the drive links before putting a newly sharpened chain back into service. If the tangs of these are worn, resharpen them with a ¼″ round file. Should the tang ends be bent up, you probably have the wrong sprocket on your saw.

After sharpening a chain off the machine, shake and brush off filings, clean the chain in solvent, and soak it briefly in No. 30 oil. Be sure to adjust chain tension according to the manufacturer's instructions before using the saw.

CHAPTER SIX

EDGED WOODWORKING TOOLS

In ADDITION to sharp saws, good woodworking demands keen knife-edged tools—chisels, planes, scrapers, jointer knives, and molding cutters. Any time one of these balks, whether it's driven by muscle or motor, better suspect dullness and do something about it. The duller an edge gets, remember, the more metal must be removed to sharpen it—and the more difficult the chore becomes.

Files can be used to sharpen a few low-carbon chisels and scrapers. But for tools of harder temper, and for that final touch that makes the difference between a fair edge and a superb one, you'll want an oilstone, plus a slipstone or two for such special tools as gouges.

For reconditioning abused edges and sharpening high-carbon tools such as jointer knives, a grinding head is desirable. It should ideally have two wheels; a 36-grit for roughing and a 60-grit wheel for finish grinding are a good choice. If you don't have a grinding head, you can mount a cup wheel on a drill press, or a straight wheel on the arbor of a table saw or a radial saw. (Remember to run the wheel within its rated speed.)

A serious drawback to grinding on the circular saw or the drill press is that neither provides a proper wheel guard. For safety's sake, always wear goggles. Also, check a grinding wheel for cracks each time you mount it, and *never* use a damaged one.

For accurate sharpening, some kind of guide is often required. It may be improvised or a purchased fixture. A blade sharpening attachment offered by Sears Roebuck and Co., for example, holds blades at any grinding angle from 25 to 40 degrees and allows them to be moved across the wheel (mounted on the arbor of a table saw) to produce accurate hollow-ground bevels. Simple shop-made grinding helps will be described farther on.

The edge you want, of course, is one that will do its intended work and stand up to it as well. The more acute the bevel angle, the keener the edge. The more obtuse the angle, the stronger the edge. Usually the original bevel angle is the best compromise between these two limits.

86

With practice, you'll be able to feel your way to a keen edge. Don't, of course, slide a finger *along* an edge—if it is sharp, it will draw blood. Instead, touch the edge in one place only, and lightly draw a finger *across* it. Try it on a dull and a sharp knife to feel the difference. Some experts judge the keenness of a chisel or a plane iron by carefully pushing the edge over the surface of a thumbnail. A poor edge slides over it or scrapes up a little powder. A sharp one can actually turn up a tiny shaving.

Fig. 1. File-sharpening a wood chisel clamped in a vise, the edge bevel horizontal.

WOOD CHISELS AND PLANE IRONS. To file wood chisels, clamp them in a vise with the edge bevel up and horizontal; the shank of the tool will be slanting up from right to left as in Figure 1. Standing on the right, file toward (that is, off) the edge, holding the file horizontal. Use a fine mill file, and finish by whetting on a bench stone as described below.

Grinding is the first step in reconditioning very dull, worn, or abused wood chisels and plane irons. Lay the blade flat on the grinding rest, bevel up, making contact with the wheel at or slightly below its center (Figure 2). Move the edge horizontally back and forth with light pressure, dipping it frequently in water or pausing long enough between passes to let it air cool. Check the edge with a try square to grind it straight and true (that is, at 90 degrees to the blade length).

Fig. 2. Grinding a dull chisel on a wheel. Move the edge back and forth, applying light pressure; dip in water or pause between passes to let blade cool.

The one exception to this is the iron of a jack plane, which should be gently rounded as in Figure 3. Note that the curve is not a full arc, but slightly larger in radius at the center. The corners are rounded to a smaller radius. The edge of a smoothing plane should be straight, but its corners should be rounded. Chisel corners should be square and sharp.

Further steps in sharpening chisels and plane irons are alike. The blade bevel is ground next. With practice, you can learn to hold the blade against the grinding wheel at the correct angle by butting the fingers of the lower hand (while gripping the blade top and bottom) against the edge of the grinding rest. But changing your grip even slightly, or its pressure against the rest, can alter the angle.

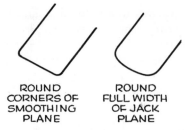

ROUND
CORNERS OF
SMOOTHING
PLANE

ROUND
FULL WIDTH
OF JACK
PLANE

Fig. 3. Comparison between blades of
a smoothing plane and a jack plane.

If you sharpen such tools only occasionally and don't have time or opportunity to develop such off-hand skill, some mechanical means of maintaining the correct angle is fully justified. The simplest is a machinist's parallel clamp tightened on the tool shank at a point where, abutted against the edge of the tool rest as in Figure 4, it will let the edge touch the wheel at an angle of 25 to 30 degrees. (Remember that grinding angles are taken from a tangent at the point of contact.)

A good homemade grinding guide or stop can be made of two flat mending plates and a couple of small bolts and wing nuts (Figure 5). One plate goes under and one on top of the blade, the nuts clamping them in the strategic position that yields the correct grinding angle when the stop is against the grinding rest, as shown in a photo.

Fig. 4. Machinist's parallel
clamp used to maintain correct
bevel angle when sharpening
chisels or plane irons.

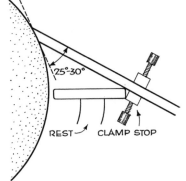

25°-30°

REST   CLAMP STOP

Check the alignment of the machinist's clamp or the mending plates with a try square to set them at exactly 90 degrees. The stop won't interfere with traversing the blade across the wheel, and if set true will produce a hollow-ground bevel at exactly 90 degrees to the blade length. It will also assure maintaining the same grinding angle no matter how often you lift the blade to dip it in water or to inspect the bevel being ground. (Remember to cool the edge frequently; a moment's forgetfulness can overheat it enough to draw its temper.)

A full bevel ground at 30 degrees will be twice as long as the blade is thick (Figure 6). The next step is grinding the edge bevel. Although you could shift the stop a trifle and do this on the grinding wheel, really keen edges call for whetting the edge bevel on a stone. It would also be possible to get a good edge by whetting the entire blade bevel, but this would be wasteful and time

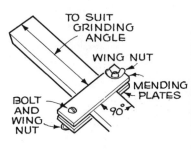

Fig. 5. Homemade stop of two flat mending plates joined with bolts and wing nuts can be used to maintain bevel angle. Photo shows it in use grinding a plane iron. The stop butts against the tool rest and holds the iron at the correct grinding angle.

consuming. Instead, the blade is whetted at a slightly more obtuse angle—about 5 degrees more—to form a second, very narrow bevel at the very edge (Figure 7). For resharpening, this small bevel can be whetted several times, until it is finally so wide that regrinding is justified.

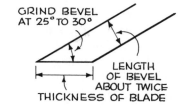

Fig. 6. Correct ratio between bevel length and blade thickness.

To whet the edge bevel by hand, grasp the blade with the fingers of both hands. Keeping the wrists rigid, move the blade over the oiled stone in either an elongated oval, or a figure-eight movement. Take special care to replace the blade on the stone at the same angle after you lift it to inspect the whetted edge. You will probably have to wipe oil off it in order to see how whetting is progressing.

One sign to look for is a wire edge that appears on the back of the blade. You can feel it (often before you can see it) by rubbing a finger over the flat

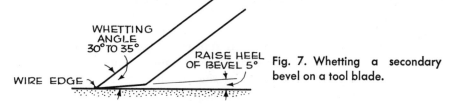

Fig. 7. Whetting a secondary bevel on a tool blade.

Remove the wire edge formed in whetting the secondary bevel by whetting the back of the blade—with a rotary motion—flat on the stone. The blade may next be stropped on leather or the palm of the hand by drawing it backwards.

of the blade. This wire edge means that whetting is almost done. Break it off by running it across the edge grain of a piece of hardwood. Then stone the edge bevel once more lightly.

Next, turn the blade over to stone its flat side lightly, holding it perfectly flat on the stone without the least tilt. As a final step, some craftsmen like to finish keen edges by stropping. You can do this on the palm of the hand or on the smooth (hair) side of a piece of leather. Strop only with a trailing stroke, of course, so as not to dig in.

In reconditioning very old or worn blades, remember that the back face must be absolutely flat to provide a good cutting edge. Deep scratches, grooves or ripples will create minute notches (and dull spots) in the edge. Whet out such defects on the coarse side of a bench stone in the same way you remove a wire edge.

A homemade whetting guide will maintain the bevel angle automatically. One such guide, shown in Figure 8 and in a photo, uses a spool roller that is adjustable for height by moving a plain and a wing nut on a long bolt. The whetting angle is set either by changing roller height this way or by shifting the blade higher or lower on the tongue. For clamping the blade on this, you can use the same mending plates suggested as a grinding guide or stop. Another guide, even simpler to make, is shown in Figure 9.

Such guides will sharpen most straight edged tools but of course won't whet the rounded edge of a jack plane. This must be done by hand. With practice you'll be able to roll the blade slightly, so as to whet all parts of its curved edge, without changing the bevel angle.

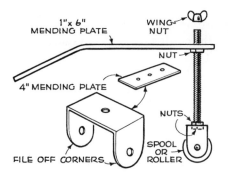

1"x 6" MENDING PLATE
WING NUT
NUT
4" MENDING PLATE
NUTS
FILE OFF CORNERS
SPOOL OR ROLLER

Fig. 8. Homemade roller guide maintains the correct whetting angle for plane irons, wood chisels, and other single-bevel tools. Mending plates clamp the blade to the tongue of the guide. Adjust the whetting angle to about 5 degrees more than the bevel angle to form the small secondary bevel. Whet until you can feel a wire edge formed on the back of the blade.

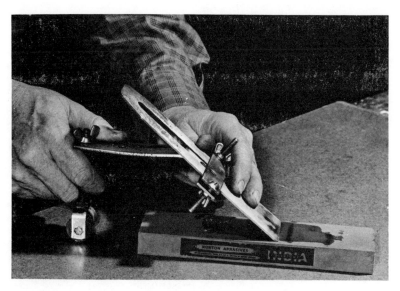

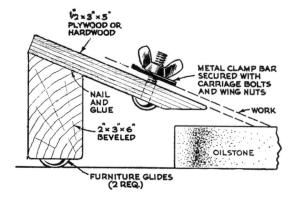

½ x 3" x 5" PLYWOOD OR HARDWOOD
METAL CLAMP BAR SECURED WITH CARRIAGE BOLTS AND WING NUTS
NAIL AND GLUE
WORK
2" x 3" x 6" BEVELED
OILSTONE
FURNITURE GLIDES (2 REQ.)

Fig. 9. Another whetting guide for maintaining the proper bevel angle. Bevel the two-by-three at about 60 degrees. With the blade bolted to the plywood strip, and the base resting on a flat surface, move blade over the stone. Furniture glides reduce friction. Length of blade overhang determines whetting angle.

Assemble plane irons with care. The cap iron must hug the blade closely and should be set only slightly back from the cutting edge, as in Figure 10. If the bottom of the cap iron is dubbed off so that it does not make full contact with the blade, chips will catch and choke up the plane. Whet the cap iron as shown in the accompanying photo to restore its flat surface.

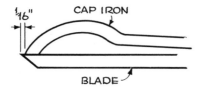

Fig. 10. Proper position of a plane's cap iron on the blade.

After assembling the plane iron and cap, see whether the cap touches the full width of the blade. If not, whet the cap by rubbing it flat on an oilstone.

WOOD-TURNING CHISELS are of tool steel, and for the strength needed to stand up to the shock of lathe work are ground with flat—not concave or hollow—bevels. You can, if they are in bad shape, do rough truing on the rim of a grinding wheel, but finish-grind the bevels flat on the side of a suitable wheel as in Figure 11.

Fig. 11. Grinding a wood-turn-ing chisel on the side of a wheel.

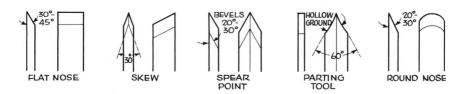

FLAT NOSE   SKEW   SPEAR POINT   PARTING TOOL   ROUND NOSE

Fig. 12. Grinding guide for correct bevel angles on wood-turning chisels. With the exception of the parting tool, all bevels are ground flat.

Flat-nose, spear-point and skew chisels that are in good condition may be sharpened entirely on the side of the wheel. (Should nicks require the removal of much metal, start grinding on the wheel rim.) Grind the bevels to the original angles or within the limits shown in Figure 12. Take care to hold the tool steady so as not to form facets or a convex bevel.

After grinding, whet the full blade bevel; don't form a secondary edge bevel as is done on ordinary wood chisels and plane irons. Whet both bevels of double-edged tools, so removing any wire edge completely. But whet only the bevel side of the flat-nose turning chisel.

Round-nose turning chisels and gouges must be rolled from side to side on the grinding wheel to make their curved edges smooth and symmetrical. Remember to finish grinding on the side of the wheel. Whet only the bevel of the round-nose tool.

To whet the edge of a gouge, apply the convex side to the concave face of a slip-stone (left) so that the rear of the bevel is clear of the stone. Form a secondary bevel by pushing the gouge forward and rotating at the same time. Then remove the wire edge by honing on the convex face of the stone (right).

Grind the bevel on the gouge to 20 degrees. Then, using a gouge slip, whet a secondary bevel of about 30 degrees on the outside. Finish by honing the inside surface on the slip, holding the gouge flat on the stone.

The parting tool is an exception in that it may profitably be hollow-ground on the wheel rim as in Figure 13. Grind each bevel to 30 degrees, so forming a 60-degree included angle on the point. If final grinding is done with light pressure, whetting may not be necessary. However, for turning smooth-bottomed grooves, the edge may be touched up with a handstone.

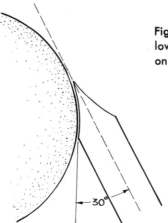

Fig. 13. Parting tool, which has hollow-ground bevels, can be sharpened on the rim of a grinding wheel.

CABINET SCRAPERS are of fairly soft steel and so may be ground, filed, or whetted. The wide edges are perhaps more easily kept square by the latter two methods. To file a square-edged cabinet scraper, clamp it in a vise with only a little of one edge projecting. With a fine mill file held horizontal but at 45 degrees to the edge, file from right to left, traversing the full width of the edge as you stroke the file forward (Figure 14).

The object is to form sharp, clean 90-degree edges on all four sides. In view of the blade's thinness, this can be done on the face of a wheel. When all nicks are gone and the edge is straight, it should be finished by draw-filing or whetting. For draw-filing, hold a fine mill file flat on the edge and straight across it, using two hands. Push the file along the edge in this position, (Figure 15) and repeat until a fine wire edge forms on each side of the blade. To whet the edges instead, hold the blade perpendicular on the edge of a bench stone held in a vise (Figure 16). Whet until fine wire edges appear.

Remove the wire edges, whether produced by whetting or by filing, by whetting the flat sides of the scraper on a fine stone as shown in Figure 17.

Now the edge must be "turned" to make an efficient scraper. Clamp the tool in a vise with about 1½″ protruding. Oil the edge. Hold a smooth steel rod, a screwdriver shank, or a ribbed burnisher made for the purpose straight across the edge at the far end, tilt one end of the rod or burnisher down about 10 degrees (Figure 18) and with fairly hard pressure draw it toward you. Repeat once with the burnishing tool tilted 15 degrees.

This should form a 15-degree hook on the edge, superficially similar to a wire edge but much stronger. Turn down the other side of this edge the same way, and repeat on all four edges. A scraper can often be resharpened simply by turning the edges again, without filing, whetting, or grinding.

Bevel-edged scrapers may be ground with a 30- to 45-degree bevel. Whet or draw-file to this angle; then whet the flat (unbeveled) side to remove the wire edge. The true edge may then be turned toward the unbeveled side with a burnisher.

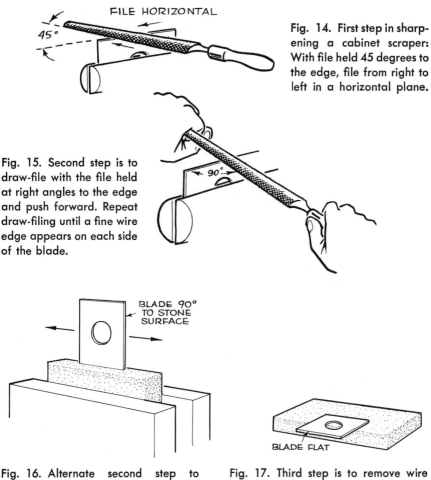

FILE HORIZONTAL

45°

Fig. 14. First step in sharpening a cabinet scraper: With file held 45 degrees to the edge, file from right to left in a horizontal plane.

Fig. 15. Second step is to draw-file with the file held at right angles to the edge and push forward. Repeat draw-filing until a fine wire edge appears on each side of the blade.

90°

BLADE 90°
TO STONE
SURFACE

BLADE FLAT

Fig. 16. Alternate second step to draw-filing is to whet edge on a bench stone until a wire edge appears.

Fig. 17. Third step is to remove wire edge by whetting scraper edges flat on a fine bench stone.

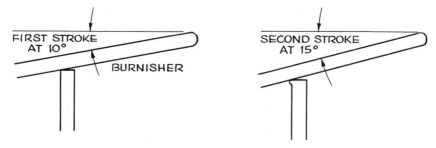

FIRST STROKE
AT 10°

BURNISHER

SECOND STROKE
AT 15°

Fig. 18. Fourth step is to "turn" the edge. After oiling the edge, draw a steel burnisher along it once at a 10-degree angle, then at a 15-degree angle. Repeat on the opposite side.

DRAWKNIVES should have perfectly straight edges, with flat or hollow-ground bevels at 30 degrees to the sides. A block clamped to the grinding rest will help keep the edge straight and maintain the bevel angle. The handles on a drawknife may interefere by striking some part of the grinder, so check this out before starting up the wheel. Check the edge with a steel rule to make sure it is ground straight.

Whet by stroking a fine stone along the bevel a few times (Figure 19). Remove the wire edge by whetting the back of the blade with the stone flat against it.

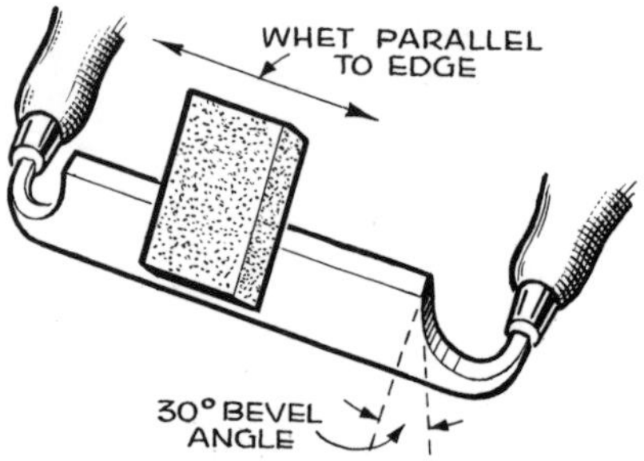

Fig. 19. Whet the bevel edge of a drawknife by stroking a fine stone along its length; then stone the back of the blade to remove the wire edge.

SPOKESHAVES have small removable blades that can be sharpened much like plane irons. A block of wood with a close-fitting kerf cut in one side for the blade will make it easier to hold. The blade bevel may be 25 to 30 degrees and hollow ground. Finish by whetting at the same angle, and remove the wire edge by rubbing the blade flat on a fine stone.

JOINTER KNIVES, if not nicked or otherwise damaged, can for a time be sharpened right on the jointer. Before this is done, and whenever the knives are removed and replaced, it is vital that they be properly set. This means that the edges are parallel to the table surfaces of the machine and all at precisely the same height. If the edges are uneven, they will do poor work and wear rapidly.

Jointer manufacturers and mail-order houses offer a knife-setting gauge for the purpose. This rests on the rear table, with an index rod touching the knife edge. You can also use a large horseshoe magnet or two bar magnets as follows (the magnets should have smoothly ground, flat surfaces):

Adjust front and rear tables to the same height. Clamp a stop block across the front table just ahead of a knife in its topmost position, and lay the magnet or magnets against the block (Figure 20). With one knife exactly at its topmost position, mark the magnet opposite the knife edge. Loosen the setscrews to let the magnet pull the blade up against it, and then retighten the screws. Repeat with the other knives, first aligning their edges with the mark on the magnet.

To whet jointer knives in the cutter head, lock one knife with its bevel parallel to the table surfaces. This can be done by clamping both sides of the belt to a wooden block. Wrap three-fourths of a flat oilstone in paper and

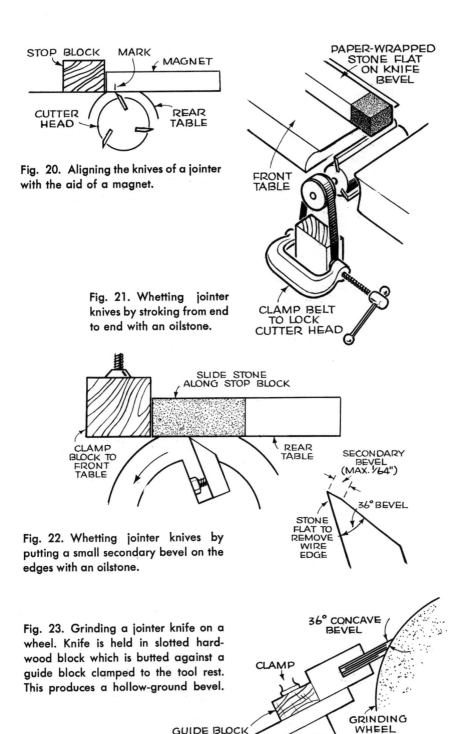

STOP BLOCK   MARK   MAGNET

CUTTER HEAD   REAR TABLE

Fig. 20. Aligning the knives of a jointer with the aid of a magnet.

PAPER-WRAPPED STONE FLAT ON KNIFE BEVEL

FRONT TABLE

CLAMP BELT TO LOCK CUTTER HEAD

Fig. 21. Whetting jointer knives by stroking from end to end with an oilstone.

SLIDE STONE ALONG STOP BLOCK

CLAMP BLOCK TO FRONT TABLE

REAR TABLE

SECONDARY BEVEL (MAX. 1/64")

36° BEVEL

STONE FLAT TO REMOVE WIRE EDGE

Fig. 22. Whetting jointer knives by putting a small secondary bevel on the edges with an oilstone.

Fig. 23. Grinding a jointer knife on a wheel. Knife is held in slotted hardwood block which is butted against a guide block clamped to the tool rest. This produces a hollow-ground bevel.

36° CONCAVE BEVEL

CLAMP

GUIDE BLOCK

GRINDING WHEEL

place the wrapped part on the front table, adjusting this so that the stone just touches the blade bevel (Figure 21).

Stroke the stone from one end of the knife to the other, counting the strokes, until a very fine wire edge turns up on the back of the blade. Lock the other stones in the same position and whet them with the same number of strokes. Then remove the wire edges with one or two strokes of a small hand-stone held flat against the back of the knives.

Another method of sharpening jointer knives in the machine is by jointing. Clamp a stop block across the front table parallel to the cutter head as in Figure 22. With the paper-wrapped stone on the rear table, cautiously lower the table until the stone makes light contact with the rotating cutter. Slide the stone once across the table; then stop the machine to inspect the edges. Joint only until all show a very narrow, bright line of equal width its full length. This is a small secondary bevel (Figure 22). When it becomes wider than $\frac{1}{64}''$, it's time to regrind the knives.

Grinding jointer knives requires some sort of blade holder, which you can make by slotting a piece of hardwood as in Figure 23. Adjust the grinding-wheel rest to form a 36-degree bevel and clamp a guide block on it, parallel to the wheel face, as shown. Adjust the block to take a very light grind only; a heavy cut will burn the blade and ruin it.

Make sure the slot in the blade holder is clean and that the blades seat fairly at the bottom. Grind all the blades in turn at the same setting. Then insert a strip of paper between blade holder and guide block for the second pass, another for a third, and so on.

Most experts, however, prefer a flat-ground bevel on jointer knives. Flat bevels can be ground on the side of a steel-backed or cup wheel provided it's large enough. One mounted on the arbor of a table saw will do a good job. A different blade holder will be needed, for saw arbors cannot be tilted sufficiently to form the 36-degree bevel with the knife flat. The holder in Figure 24 can be slid along the fence, paper being inserted for successive passes. A similar setup can be used for grinding on a belt, disk sander, or radial-arm saw.

With the same blade holder tilted 90 degrees to hold the knife bevels up and horizontal, jointer knives can be ground on a drill press. A cup wheel should be used, the blade holder being slid under it against a fence strip clamped to the table as in Figure 25.

If you want to go to the trouble of building a cradle as shown in Figure 26, you can grind the knives right in the cutter head. On the jointer, insert a block between each blade and the front table to index three saw cuts on the pulley edge. An indexing strip on the cradle will then hold each knife in turn with its bevel up for grinding. Slide the cradle along a fence strip.

After grinding, whatever method is used, take off the wire edges by stoning the back of each knife lightly. Be sure to set the knives accurately in the cutter head before using the machine. Once jointer knives have been ground so far back that the setscrews no longer bear fully against them, discard them for new knives. A narrow knife might pull free and fly off with terrific force.

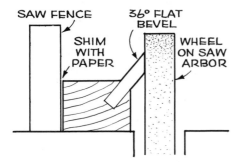

SAW FENCE

SHIM WITH PAPER

36° FLAT BEVEL

WHEEL ON SAW ARBOR

Fig. 24. Flat-ground bevels can be formed by grinding jointer knives on the side of a steel-backed or cup wheel mounted on a table saw. Wooden block, slotted to hold knife at a 36-degree angle, is pushed along the fence.

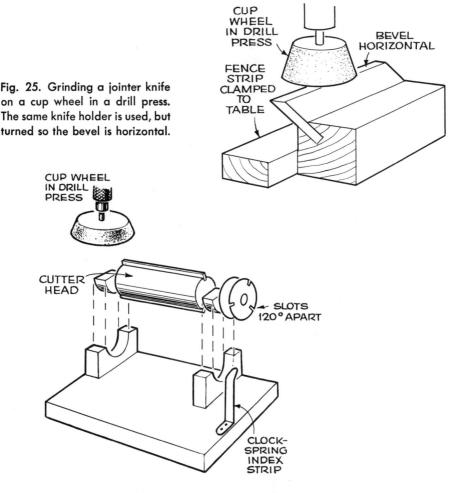

CUP WHEEL IN DRILL PRESS

BEVEL HORIZONTAL

FENCE STRIP CLAMPED TO TABLE

Fig. 25. Grinding a jointer knife on a cup wheel in a drill press. The same knife holder is used, but turned so the bevel is horizontal.

CUP WHEEL IN DRILL PRESS

CUTTER HEAD

SLOTS 120° APART

CLOCK-SPRING INDEX STRIP

Fig. 26. Jointer knives can be sharpened in the cutter head with this homemade cradle. The clock-spring index strip catches in slots sawed in the pulley, holding the cutter head in position with the knife bevels horizontal.

MOLDING-HEAD CUTTERS have a single bevel, which should be flat rather than hollow-ground. As all three blades must be of exactly equal length, it's recommended that you make a hardwood step jig as shown in Figure 27 to hold them for simultaneous sharpening. Stack the blades so that the bevels form a continuous line and measure the depth of the steps necessary. Bottom each blade firmly in the jig and clamp all together, taking care that the sides are parallel and the beveled molding edges line up.

The jig is no guarantee of good work in itself, however. In grinding, the blades must be presented to the wheel at the precise angle that will grind each to the same depth, an angle equal to that of the steps. Straight or planer blades can be ground this way on the side of the wheel.

Curved edges are more safely sharpened by filing. Lock the stacked blades in a vise with the three bevels horizontal (Figure 28). File *into* the edges only, lifting the file on the return stroke, and be careful to hold the file horizontal, so maintaining the original bevel angle precisely. The hard steel requires firm pressure and sharp files. Use flat, triangular, or round fine-cut files as necessary to suit the molding contour, and file only until the edges are sharp.

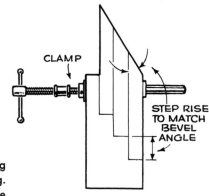

CLAMP

STEP RISE
TO MATCH
BEVEL
ANGLE

Fig. 27. Hardwood jig for holding molding-head cutters for grinding. Steps in the jig are cut so as to hold the cutters with their bevel angles aligned.

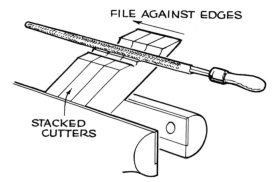

FILE AGAINST EDGES

STACKED
CUTTERS

Fig. 28. To file the curved edges of molding-head cutters, lock the cutters in a vise with their bevel angles horizontal and file *into* the edges only.

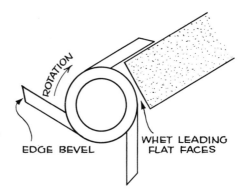

Fig. 29. Sharpening three-wing shaper cutters.

ROTATION

EDGE BEVEL

WHET LEADING
FLAT FACES

If molding cutters need only touching up, their intricate edges are best sharpened with gouge slips and small abrasive files. Small mounted wheels, driven in a high-speed hand grinder, may also be used.

To shape your own cutters from straight-edged ones, use a wheel dresser to round off the wheel face for grinding concave shapes. Do as much shaping of the cutters on the side of the wheel as possible, however, to grind flat rather than hollow-ground bevels. Finish by filing as described above, always filing into or against the edges so as to form no wire edges.

Finally, compare the cutters to make sure all are of the same length. A slight difference may be corrected by stoning the opposite end of over-long cutters.

THREE-WING SHAPER CUTTERS (Figure 29) are best sharpened by whetting the flat faces adjacent to the edges. This can be done with a hand-stone, on a bench stone, or on a fine-grit grinding wheel. Whetting these faces will not alter the contour of the three edges, which must be precisely alike. To grind the edges properly would require a shaped grinding wheel, an arbor on which the cutter can be held against the wheel, and some means of locking each edge in turn in the same grinding position.

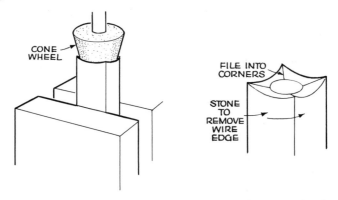

CONE WHEEL

FILE INTO CORNERS

STONE TO REMOVE WIRE EDGE

Fig. 30. Cone-shaped grinding wheel mounted in a drill press is best bet for sharpening a mortising chisel. Finish by filing inside corners with a triangular file, then stone the sides to remove the wire edges.

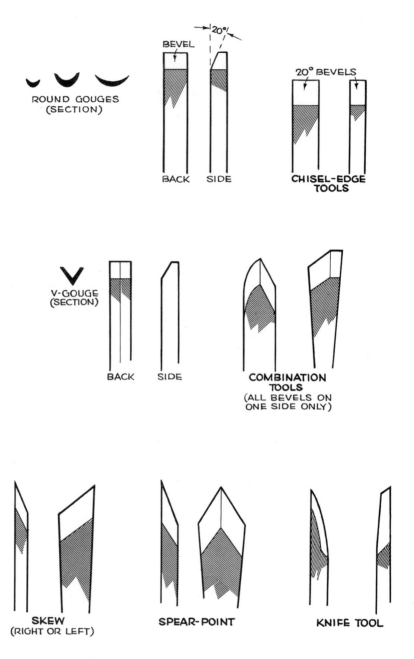

ROUND GOUGES
(SECTION)

BEVEL

20°

BACK   SIDE

20° BEVELS

CHISEL-EDGE
TOOLS

V-GOUGE
(SECTION)

BACK   SIDE

COMBINATION
TOOLS
(ALL BEVELS ON
ONE SIDE ONLY)

SKEW
(RIGHT OR LEFT)

SPEAR-POINT

KNIFE TOOL

Fig. 31. These are the basic tools used in wood carving. Requiring very keen edges, they should be sharpened with a fine-grained, hard stone. Bevel angles shown are for guidance in regrinding, which should be done only if the edge or bevel is badly abused. Grind these tools on a fine-grained wheel.

MORTISING CHISELS are a combination of knife-edged and rotary tools. The spurless auger bit can be sharpened as described in a following chapter, but the chisel is a special case. It is square, with four cutting edges beveled on the inside only.

A cone-shaped mounted wheel of appropriate size, chucked in a drill press, makes sharpening fairly easy. The chisel can be clamped vertically in a drill-press vise and the rotating grinding wheel fed against it, or the chisel can be fed upward against the wheel by hand. This will grind a flat bevel inside the four edges (Figure 30).

When the bevel is ground true to the edges, clamp the chisel in a vise and sharpen the four inside corners with a small triangular file. Be careful not to lower the outside corners; leave a single sharp point at each. As a last step, rub each of the four sides flat on a fine stone to whet off the wire edges left by the grinding wheel.

CARVING TOOLS come in a variety of shapes, some of them similar to those of wood-turning chisels though much smaller. Gouges come in several sizes, as do veining or V-gouge tools. Although typical bevel angles are shown in Figure 31, they are for guidance in regrinding rather than sharpening.

These tools require very keen edges. Sharpen them with a fine-grained, hard stone such as an Arkansas file or slip. Follow the original bevel angles closely. Regrind the bevels only if the edge or bevel is badly abused or so worn as to require it. Grind on a fine-grained wheel. If the wheel is of fairly large diameter (5″ or 6″) the bevels may be hollow ground. On smaller wheels, grind bevels flat on the wheel side. Whet the bevels; then stone the backs carefully (or the inside of gouges) to remove any wire edge.

CHAPTER SEVEN

SHARPENING THE TOOLS THAT MAKE HOLES

HOLE-MAKING tools are vital to anyone who makes or repairs things. They are also probably the least understood of all common tools. Topping the list is the ordinary twist drill. To sharpen it properly, it is first necessary to understand its anatomy and the reasons for its structure.

Examine a twist drill, and you'll find two spiral lands (or ridges) around a solid central web. Inversely, one could say the drill is a rod with two spiral grooves or flutes in it. At the point, the lands are ground to form an included angle of 118 degrees—that is, each point surface is at 59 degrees to the axis of the drill. Where the point surfaces meet at the center, they form a chisel edge (Figure 1).

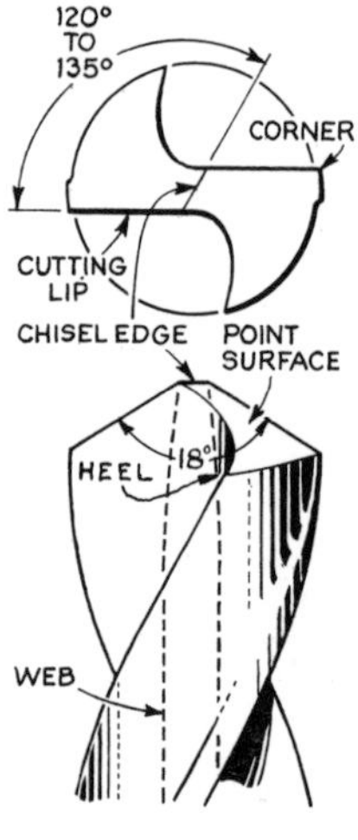

Fig. 1. Spiral lands of a twist drill form an included angle at the point of 118 degrees. Point surfaces form a chisel edge where they meet at the center.

The point surfaces must not be those of a true cone. If they are (and on many an improperly sharpened drill they turn out that way) the drill will simply turn on the work like a shaft on a cone bearing. Sharp as the edges (or cutting lips) may be, they cannot penetrate because all parts of the point surfaces bear on the work equally at the same time. To let the drill work, only the very edge of the cutting lips must touch. The rest of the point surfaces must be ground back slightly to leave clearance (Figure 2).

To grind such point surfaces, you cannot simply turn the drill as you would a center punch (which has a true cone point). Instead, you must change the grinding angle as you grind from lip to heel, forming surfaces that spiral inward slightly. On the drill this can be seen as the clearance angle.

Fig. 2. Point surfaces of a twist drill must be ground back slightly so that only the cutting lips bear on the work.

HOW TWIST DRILLS WEAR. The outer corners of the cutting lips, which move fastest and take out the most material, are first to wear. They round off slightly, and in this condition they begin to drill undersize. This transfers a heavy burden to the flute edges, which are pinched in the hole, generating much heat. This softens the metal and further speeds up wear.

At the same time, wear on the cutting lips also forms a slight flat on them, areas which have the configuration of a true cone and therefore no clearance. These flats keep the edges from cutting, rub in the hole, and generate still more heat to round out the vicious circle.

This sequence points up the importance of timely sharpening. Drilling by power often camouflages the dullness of a drill for a time. By feeding a little harder, it makes the hole, whereupon it is easy to pass on to other matters and forget the momentary difficulty. But the drill will be even duller the next time it's used, and continued use can ruin it permanently.

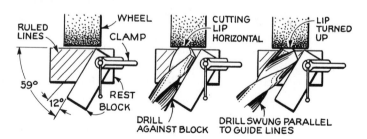

Fig. 3. Sharpening a twist drill on a grinding wheel. Clamp guide block on tool rest at an angle of 59 degrees to the wheel surface and draw a few lines on the rest 47 degrees to the wheel surface (left). Hold the drill against the block and start grinding with the cutting lip horizontal (center). Swing the drill parallel to the lines, rotating it clockwise at the same time (right). Then turn drill halfway and grind from the other cutting lip.

Twist drill being held against guide block at the start of sharpening on the side of a cup wheel. Pencil lines on the tool rest serve as a guide as drill is swung to the left and rotated clockwise.

SHARPENING TWIST DRILLS FREEHAND takes practice and patience. Trying it haphazardly, and without a grinding rest, will almost surely leave the drill unusable. A grinding rest is the first requisite. You'll get good results much sooner if you clamp a guide block to it as shown in a photo and in Figure 3. Locate the block at an angle of 59 degrees to the grinding-wheel surface, whether you use the rim or the side of the wheel. (A steel-backed or a cup wheel should be used if much side grinding is to be done.)

If you use a belt sander, the belt should be of a moderately fine grit and in good condition so that it runs flat. Mount a thick elevating block on the table to provide clearance for your hands to manipulate the drill. Fix the guide block to this clearance block at 59 degrees to the belt surface.

The guide block establishes the included angle at the cutting lips (twice 59, or 118 degrees). In front of the guide block, draw a few lines at 47 degrees to the abrasive surface of wheel or belt—12 degrees less than the lip angle.

If possible, start by sharpening a ⅜″ or larger drill for your first attempt. Begin grinding with one cutting lip horizontal (parallel to the table) and touching the wheel, the drill shank firmly against the guide block. As soon as sparks fly, start twisting the drill slowly clockwise and simultaneously swing it on the grinding rest, away from the guide block, toward the angle of the scribed lines.

Time these two movements—rotating and swinging the drill—so that you finish grinding at the heel when the drill is fully parallel to the 47-degree lines. Turn the drill over halfway and grind the same way from the second cutting lip, again starting with this horizontal.

Use moderate pressure only; unless a drill is in very bad condition indeed, it should not be necessary to remove much metal. Grind from the two lip positions alternately, and so far as possible with the same pressure and for the same length of time to keep the grinding effort on both point surfaces equal. If much metal has to be removed, let the drill air cool between grindings instead of dipping it in water. Be sure to grind a smooth, continuous surface behind each cutting lip, without flats or nicks.

Lip lengths must be equal. So must lip angles, though this should be assured by the guide block. A drill gauge (Figure 4) is best for checking. You can make the gauge of cardboard, though thin sheet steel will make it much more durable. Figures may be added to the markings to make it easier for you to remember and compare readings. The drawing shows how the drill is held to measure lip lengths, then turned to check clearance at the heel.

With a guide block, you aren't likely to grind the lips at different angles, but by grinding more on one point surface than the other, you may make the cutting lips of unequal length. When this is the case, the drill will make an oversize hole (which can be anathema in some machining operations) and will wear rapidly. Checking lip lengths against a gauge (with a magnifying glass if need be) is best. But for a rough check, you can turn the drill by hand into a bar of soap. If it turns up chips of equal length in both flutes, the lips are reasonably close to the same size. The acid test is to drill a hole in metal (preferably on a drill press to insure against any wobbling of the drill) and then see how well the shank end of the drill fits the hole. If it is a sloppy fit, the drill is working oversize.

Seen from the end, the chisel tip should form an angle of 120 to 135 degrees with the cutting lips as in Figure 1. If the angle is much different from

Fig. 4. Drill gauge used to check lip length of a twist drill.

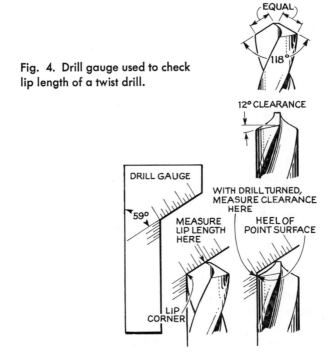

CHISEL EDGE
TOO WIDE

GRIND HERE
TO THIN WEB

Fig. 5

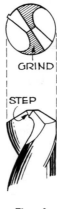

GRIND

STEP

Fig. 6

GRIND A
VERTICAL FLAT
FOR BRASS

Fig. 7

this, check your clearance angles too. The 118-degree point angle is standard for most work, but a blunter 150-degree angle is sometimes used for very hard materials, while a 90- or 100-degree point may be recommended for cast iron and copper respectively, and a still more acute 60-degree point is sometimes ground on drills to be used in wood, bakelite, fiber, and other relatively soft materials.

When the chisel edge becomes wider than normal, it's because the drill has been ground back to a point at which the web is thicker (see Figure 1, which shows how the web tapers near the point). This overlong chisel edge demands a lot of extra power and feed pressure, both of which overheat the drill and shorten its useful life. Web thinning is therefore an important part of reconditioning drills larger than $\frac{3}{16}''$.

It can be done on a straight, rounded, or cutoff wheel, or with a small mounted wheel in a hand grinder as shown in a photo. The simplest method (Figure 5) is to grind inside each flute from a point halfway along the cutting lip, and far enough up the flute to merge gradually into the thicker web section. A distance equal to one half to one third of the drill's diameter is about right. Keep the cutting lip straight, blending the ground area smoothly into the curve of the adjacent flute.

Another method of web thinning is to grind what machinists call an offset or crankshaft point (because such drills are often used for drilling oil holes in crankshafts). As Figure 6 shows, this can be done on the corner of a straight wheel, for it consists of grinding two angled flats at the heels of the point surfaces. In place of the chisel edge, this forms two short secondary edges that penetrate more easily.

Larger drills especially tend to "hog in" or catch and grab when drilling brass or bronze. This can be avoided by grinding small vertical flats (parallel to the drill axis) at each cutting lip as in Figure 7. This prevents seizing, but unfortunately it makes the drill unsuitable for steel and other metals, and regrinding to the depth of the flat wastes a lot of the drill's useful length. Many mechanics prefer not to alter their drills this way, but instead reduce feed and speed to minimize the chance of seizing. To do so, it's quite as important that the work itself be firmly held down as that the drill be fed with caution.

DRILL-GRINDING ATTACHMENTS. These devices hold the drill at the proper angle, and theoretically control the depth to which you grind, while you swing it to produce the not-quite-conical point surfaces and the clearance angles. The attachments can be adjusted to grind the four most useful point angles—49, 59, 68, and 88 degrees. A screw adjustment advances the drill against the wheel between grinding passes.

The attachments must be used with judgment nevertheless. Setting up the drill in the lip guide that positions it is a critical and far from foolproof operation; a small error can result in faulty sharpening, with insufficient or even reversed clearance angles, or a misaligned chisel edge. Also, too much hand pressure can result in grinding one point surface more than the other, forming unequal lip lengths.

Carefully used, however, these devices can do a good job of sharpening ⅛″ and larger drills. One, made by General Hardware Manufacturing Corp. for hardware store distribution and also sold by Sears, Roebuck and Co., forms both the correct point angles and the clearance angles as you sweep the drill against the wheel side. A cheaper attachment, made by A. D. McBurney, Los Angeles, forms both the correct point angles and clearance angles as you sweep the drill against the wheel side, as shown in the photos on the next page. This attachment also allows you to form a rounded point by sliding the drill up by hand and grinding a little more off the heel.

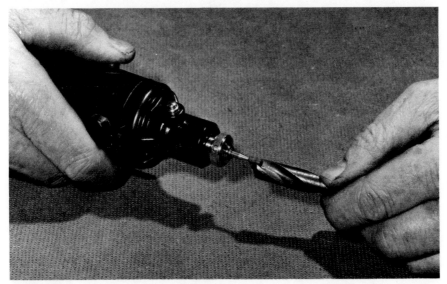

Thinning down an overly thick drill web is a delicate grinding job. One convenient way is with a high-speed hand grinder. A tiny cylinder wheel gets between the flutes easily.

Automatic sharpening guide holds the bit while you swing it against the wheel, providing the correct point and clearance angles in a single motion. It takes careful setting up, however.

This guide, set up here for sharpening a drill on a belt sander, establishes correct lip angle but does not grind the clearance automatically. This you do by hand.

SHARPENING SMALLER DRILLS is a somewhat more difficult job, requiring restraint (to avoid grinding too far) and a magnifying glass to check the results. You can simplify the task of grinding drills smaller than ⅛″ and still get fairly good results as follows:

Instead of rotating the drill from lip to heel as described above, hold it at a fixed angle that will form the right point and clearance angle simultaneously. The point surfaces will be flat instead of curved, but on small drills the difference is so slight that it has little effect on the strength of the edge. Hold the drill at 59 degrees to the grinding surface (as seen from above) but lower the back end of the drill about 12 degrees from the horizontal. Make sure the cutting lip is horizontal; if it is turned even a trifle, the clearance angle will be off. The necessary down tilt may be achieved by tilting the grinding rest, or the ingenious mechanic might cobble up a metal block, with a groove for the drill, to hold it at the correct compound angle (as suggested on page 33).

With care, it's also possible to sharpen very small drills (right down to No. 60) with a hand slip. Rest the drill with one flute against a sharp table or bench edge, its length sloping downward to the left. Hold the abrasive stone (a triangular hard Arkansas file, for example) tilted downward beyond the drill point and pointed to the left. Stone the point surfaces flat, counting equal strokes on both. It may be easier to get the hang of it by using a big drill first to establish the proper angles and see what you are doing.

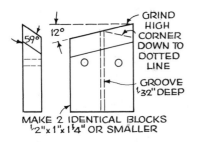

Fig. 8. Homemade steel jig is an aid in sharpening small twist drills with a handstone.

A little jig that does a much more accurate job is shown in Figure 8. Make it of steel, first squaring up two blocks to precisely the same size. Down the center of both file a small groove, using a small triangular file. The important angled face of each block is a lengthy filing job; it can be done more quickly and accurately on a sanding disk or belt, by making use of the sliding miter gauge in the table slot. Set the gauge at 59 degrees to the abrasive surface. Tilt the table down 12 degrees.

If the gauge head is not close to the abrasive, insert a piece of smooth bar stock to help support the work as near the belt or disk as possible. Use a medium-coarse abrasive paper. Grind the slope clear across the block. Then grind off the high corner, but only until it just nicks the groove.

The blocks will get very hot in the process, and should be cooled in water frequently for easy handling. Note that the two blocks are exactly alike, not right and left-handed, and that the grooves are in the faces on the high side of the slope.

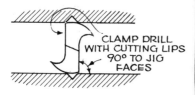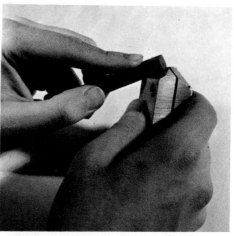

CLAMP DRILL
WITH CUTTING LIPS
90° TO JIG
FACES

Fig. 9. To use jig for stoning a twist drill, clamp the drill between the grooved faces with cutting lips aligned as shown. Keep the stone flat against the jig surface. Don't unclamp the drill until both point surfaces have been stoned flush. Sharpening can also be done on a fine wheel, but handstoning a tiny drill takes only minutes and causes less wear on the jig.

Lay a small drill in the grooves to align the two blocks, and clamp them together, their tops (that is, the ends of the grooves) at the same height. Then drill two No. 36 holes through both blocks at once. Separate the blocks, and in one tap these holes 6-32. In the other, open the holes to clearance size (drill No. 28). The blocks can now be clamped together with 6-32 bolts.

Lock the drill in the grooves this way, using a magnifying glass to set the cutting lips at right angles to the block faces as in Figure 9. (Clean the drills first, for chips in the flutes make it difficult to see the lips clearly.) The drill point should protrude very slightly above the blocks. Tighten the bolts equally so that the grooved faces are parallel.

Use a small, fine-grained stone. A large stone cannot be manipulated as precisely, for its overhanging weight will tend to lift it off the sloping guide faces. Apply finger pressure to the stone directly over the jig face. After a few strokes, examine the drill to see how sharpening is progressing. When the entire point surface has been whetted, do the second surface on the other side of the jig.

This should automatically form the chisel edge and clearance angles correctly. If it does not, the drill was probably not aligned correctly in the jig, or the block faces were not parallel.

Although the jig can be used for sharpening drills on a fine grinding wheel, handstoning is recommended instead. A wheel will wear the guide faces much more rapidly, and the point surfaces of small drills are so tiny that a handstone works surprisingly fast. It takes only four or five minutes to regrind a mangled small drill point with a handstone.

If you want to sharpen drills right down to No. 80, make an extra jig or two, with grooves to suit. A groove large enough to hold a $\frac{3}{32}''$ drill won't hold the tiniest ones, and conversely a very small groove cannot readily align the larger drills.

TIPS ON USING TWIST DRILLS. A good lubricant, though no substitute for sharp drills, reduces wear on the drills and gives you more service from them before resharpening is necessary. High-speed-steel drills will profit from lubricant too. Although they will withstand overheating better than carbon drills, they are not immune to abuse.

If you have to use a drill that needs web thinning, you can relieve the load on it and make it work faster by drilling a small pilot hole for it to follow. Use a pilot drill slightly smaller than the width of the web.

Fig. 10. File the spurs of an auger bit on the inside only, near the edges.

SHARPENING AUGER BITS. You can do this with 4" or 5" square, half-round and taper warding files or with an auger-bit stone or a small triangular abrasive file. To keep the bit boring its designated size, never file or whet its outer diameter. Sharpen the spurs by filing them on the inside only, near their edges (Figure 10). Check their shape with the spurs on a new bit, and file as close to the original shape as you can.

The cutting edges shouldn't be touched on the underside (the point side), but filed or whetted only on top, in the throat or twist of the bit, as shown in Figure 11. Take care not to undercut the screw point where it joins the cutting edges; a half-round file may be used here to preserve the radius. File a bevel on both cutting lips, and be sure you file them equally; if one lip is filed too far back, it will stand above the other and do all the work. After file sharpening, a little whetting with a fine stone will make the edges keener.

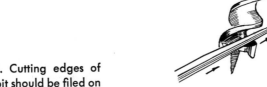

Fig. 11. Cutting edges of auger bit should be filed on top spurs from inside only.

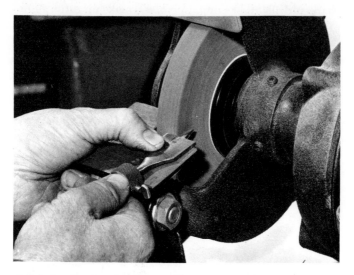

Spade bit fitted with a stop collar is easily sharpened by simply advancing it until the stop bears against the edge of the rest. Flipping it over then puts identical grind on the other side.

WOOD-BORING SPADE BITS are very popular for use in electric drills, but a dull bit can overload and even damage the drill motor. Most wing or spade bits may be either filed or ground, except for the hardened nail-cutting type, which must be ground. With a simple grinding stop, grinding is more accurate than filing. The stop may be a collar or thick ring, with a hole large enough to slide on the drill shank, and a setscrew for tightening it. A photo shows how such a ring stop is used.

The mending-plate stop shown in Chapter 4 is also practical. With either stop, set the grinding rest to produce an 8-degree bevel when the bit is laid

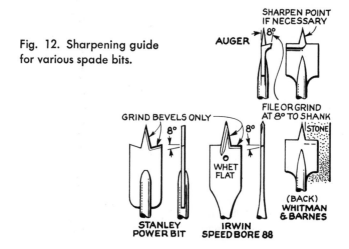

Fig. 12. Sharpening guide for various spade bits.

flat on it, as shown in the photo and in Figure 12. The wheel should turn into the edge, the bit bevel being down, to minimize burr. When one edge has been ground, the bit need only be flipped over to grind the other to the same depth. Any slight burr is easily removed by whetting the adjacent face with a stone held perfectly flat against it.

A stop insures grinding both lips to identical length. Set it to grind only a little metal off the bit; unless the edges are damaged, no more should be nec-

Fig. 13. Sharpening guide for Stanley power bore bit.

essary. If the edges are at a more acute angle than 90 degrees, as in one of the bits shown, hold the shank accordingly to grind both at the same angle. The bevels on the points can be ground, if necessary, to the same 8-degree angle by swinging the bit around about 90 degrees on the tilted grinding rest. Be sure to keep the point centered by grinding both sides equally.

Figure 13 shows how to sharpen a popular power auger bit. Having only one spur, one edge, and a plain unthreaded point, it is easier to sharpen than an ordinary auger bit.

FLY-CUTTER BITS are similar to lathe bits, and require the same rake and clearance angles for free cutting. As shown in Figure 14, the same bit can cut with the bevel inside or out depending on how it is fastened in the bar. Sharpen the bit by grinding or whetting the bevels, taking care to keep them flat.

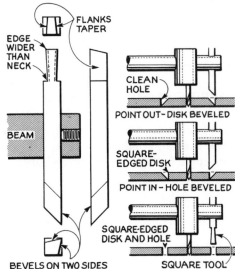

Fig. 14. Sharpening guide for fly-cutter bit, which may be ground with a bevel at one end and a square-nose at the other.

To cut a square-edged hole and disk at one time, use a square-nosed tool as shown in the drawing. The edge must be slightly wider than the neck, and both flanks must slope back to provide clearance. The same bit may be ground square at one end and to a bevel edge at the other.

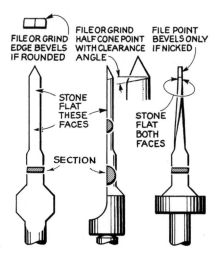

Fig. 15. Sharpening guide for three types of screw-pilot drills.

SCREW-PILOT DRILLS, which have to make relatively deep holes, wear most at the entering edges. Figure 15 shows the three most common types, one flat on both sides, another of half-round section, and the third flat at the end but twisted along the shank. Use a magnifying glass to see whether the entering edges have been rounded by wear. If not, whet the flat faces only.

Flat whetting may be done by moving a small stone over the tool surface or, perhaps more easily, by rubbing the pilot drill on a larger stone, with firm finger pressure to hold it down.

Should it be necessary to grind the bevels, do this by hand whetting only to minimize the change in diameter. In sharpening the point, take pains to keep it centered. The point of the half-round type requires the same kind of clearance as a twist drill.

CARBIDE MASONRY BITS should not be used after the edges dull, for they are then much more vulnerable to breakage. The popular type has a flat inset blade with a V-point, ground with a small end clearance back of each edge. You can grind such bits on a silicon-carbide wheel. Take care to grind both edges to the same length, and to maintain the clearance angle that allows them to work.

CHAPTER EIGHT

THE TOOLS YOU'RE LIKELY TO FORGET

WHEN did you last think of reconditioning your home or shop screwdrivers, chisels, or tin snips? These and others are tools we tend to use with little or no thought for their condition, yet in time they like any others become the worse for wear. Regrinding (which may or may not include sharpening) can not only make such tools more efficient but also safer and more pleasant to use.

SCREWDRIVERS. Strictly speaking, one doesn't sharpen a screwdriver. But when its bit is worn rounded or convex, it can slip out of a screw slot all too readily, sometimes with devastating effect on knuckles and temper. Reshaping the blade tip can make a tremendous difference in the way it grips a screw.

Seen from its side, or in profile, a screwdriver bit should have parallel sides at least to the depth to which it sinks in a screw slot. If instead the tip tapers toward the end, it will tend to rise up out of the slot when torque is applied. This tapered shape (shown at A in Figure 1) is found on some cheap screwdrivers.

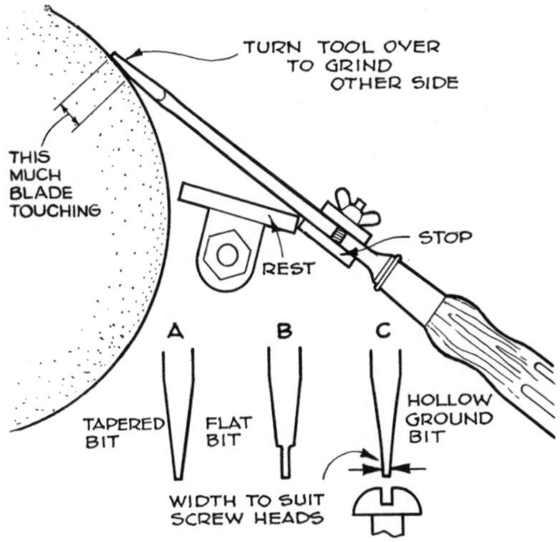

Fig. 1. Reshaping a screwdriver blade to put a hollow grind on the tip.

Grinding the faces flat with a step in each as at B gives the bit a better hold but also weakens it. Hollow grinding on a wheel forms concave faces (as at C) that are much stronger.

If the tip is nicked, rounded in either direction (that is, edgewise or flat) or out of square, first grind it straight across and at exactly 90 degrees to its shank. Do this with the grinding rest at center height, removing no more metal than you have to.

Now stop the wheel, place the screwdriver on the grinding rest with the tip high up on the wheel, and judge by sight where to hold it to hollow-grind the tip so that its end is parallel for a short distance back. To hold this angle when grinding, butt your thumb and forefinger against the edge of the grinding rest as you grasp the shank, or else clamp on a stop like the one described in Chapter 6.

With the thumb of the other hand, press the flat of the bit squarely against the wheel as in the photo, taking care not to push on one side more than on the other. When a hollow-ground surface appears across the full width of the bit, turn the screwdriver over. With the stop (or your fingers) at the same place on the shank, grind the other face. The thickness of the tip should, of course, match the size of the blade and the screw slots it is meant to enter.

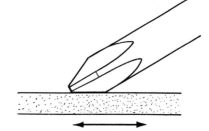

Fig. 2. Stoning the flats of a Phillips screwdriver.

Some mechanics prefer to grind the bit faces on the side of the wheel, squaring the tip off afterwards. The grinding marks left crosswise of the blade are thought to give it a slight "nonskid" surface and a better grip in screw slots. But it is more difficult to grind the ends of the tip faces parallel this way.

Screwdriver bits can also be ground square on a coarse bench stone (the shank being held at 90 degrees to the stone and whetted in this position). The faces can then be whetted with the blade flat near the edge of the stone. Try to make them parallel for $\frac{1}{16}$" back from the tip on medium-size blades.

A belt sander will do a good job of hollow-grinding screwdriver bits too. With a medium to fine belt in place, hold the bit on the high side of a belt pulley. It's best to work on the rear pulley, or to reverse the motor if you work on the front pulley, so that in either case the belt is moving away from the bit edge, or trailing. If the belt runs into the edge, it may surprise you unpleasantly by catching on it and being ripped to ribbons.

Phillips screwdrivers. The four lands on these bits may become nicked or deformed with use. The safest way to remove such damage is to stone the flats

(Figure 2) by hand, or on a fine wheel. Remove as little metal as possible. If the point is so marred that it fails to enter the screw recess, reshape it with a square-edged stone working in the flutes.

SHARPENING POINTED TOOLS, such as punches, scribers, and icepicks, can readily be done on a bench stone or even a pocket stone. Turn the tool between the fingers while stroking it along the stone, the shank being tilted up to form the desired point angle (Figure 3).

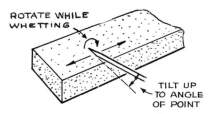

Fig. 3. Sharpening the point of a scriber.

A fine-grit wheel will resharpen pointed tools in a jiffy. Besides forming the correct angle, it's important to keep the point on center, so keep turning the tool so long as it's in contact with the wheel. A moment's hesitation can form an undesirable flat, besides throwing the point off center. The point can simply be laid on the rest, or you may find a clamped-on notched rest preferable (Figure 4). The notch makes it a bit easier to maintain the grinding angle. It's best, of course, to resharpen the point to its original angle because this minimizes grinding effort and saves metal.

A center punch to be used for layout work may have a relatively acute 60-degree point; one for punching drill starts, on the other hand, should be about 90 degrees. Besides making the point stronger, this makes a larger dimple for starting the drills. Scribers must have a relatively long, acute point. It's easy enough to form this, but there is danger of overgrinding and overheating if you use a wheel. Icepicks too are slender and readily damaged by careless grinding.

Dividers shouldn't be ground unless they are badly damaged. Ordinarily they can be sharpened to an excellent point by rubbing them with a small slipstone. Inspect them with a magnifying glass as whetting progresses.

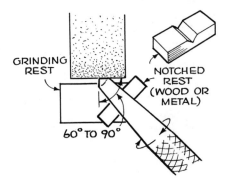

Fig. 4. Notched rest used to sharpen the point of a center punch on a grinding wheel.

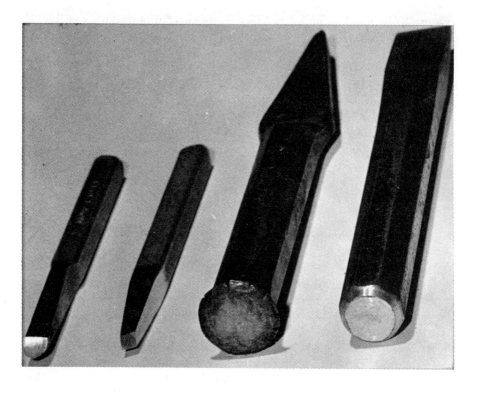

Round-nose and diamond chisels (two at left) have a single bevel only. The cape chisel (third from left) has a dangerously mushroomed split head. The flat chisel to the right of it had a similar head, which was ground off and beveled.

COLD CHISELS are among the most abused tools in the average kit. Dull edges are an obvious fault, but even more dangerous are mushroomed heads.

The quickest way to recondition edges is to grind them on a good wheel. Square the edges across first, if necessary. Then clamp a stop to the chisel body, at a distance which will bring the edge in contact with the wheel to form the desired bevel angle. The harder the metal the chisel is to cut, the blunter the edge should be. For average work, an included angle of 60 degrees is useful. For copper or brass, a 40-degree point is sometimes recommended, while for hard materials a 70-degree angle forms a stronger edge.

With a stop clamped to it, a common flat or cross-cut chisel having two edge bevels is ground on both sides simply by flipping it over against the wheel. If more than a little grinding is necessary, dip the chisel in water occasionally. Round-nose and diamond-point chisels have single bevels. For cutting soft metals, these bevels may be hollow-ground on the face of the wheel. But for heavy-duty on steels, the edges will stand up better if these chisels are ground flat on the side of the wheel.

Grinding is not necessary in every case. A chisel in good condition but blunted slightly can be resharpened by judicious handstoning.

Chisel heads that are mushroomed, or that have split around the edge, are a menace to the user. This deformed metal is brittle. The very next hammer blow may send steel slivers flying. So grind off the mushroomed part all around. Then grind a uniform bevel all around the head. The bevel prolongs the intervals between mushrooming.

COMMON SNIPS

PIVOT-
BOLT
HOLE

20° TO 25°
BEVEL
ANGLE

CUTTING
FACE

SHEAR FACE

5° BEVEL
ANGLE

PIVOT LINE

SHEAR FACE

SHEAR FACE

DUCKBILL
SNIPS

SHEAR FACE

Fig. 5. Tin snips, both the common and duckbill types, have flat shear faces and beveled edges. Grind the shear face on a flat belt or on the side of a wheel; then grind the edge bevel until it meets the shear face.

TIN SNIPS are in effect heroic scissors, and may be sharpened in much the same way—on a wheel, on a belt sander, or with a handstone. Give the blades a 20- to 25-degree bevel angle. Whet the shear faces very little—only enough to remove any burr, unless long wear shows its effect on both the edges and the top of the shear faces (Figure 5).

These are usually flat rather than hollow ground. To regrind them, the snips will have to be taken apart. Grind the faces on a flat belt or on the side of an appropriate wheel. The ground area should extend to the cutting edge and over the entire pivot area. Grind the edge bevel next, until it meets the shear face. Whet off any burr with a handstone.

Tin snips can be sharpened on a belt sander without taking the blades apart. First, tilt the sander table to the desired bevel angle and hold the snips down firmly, or use a wood block to tilt up the blade. Open the snips as far as possible to keep the other blade away from the belt. When one blade has been sharpened, turn the snips upside down to grind the other one. Finally, whet the shear (inside) face, holding a fine handstone flat on it. This will remove any burrs.

Adjust the pivot bolt so that the shear faces are held closely but not over-tightly together. Oil the joint well; it carries a heavy load in cutting.

Duckbill and other snips intended for cutting curved lines have very narrow shear faces. They are ground the same way, but be careful not to overgrind at the end where they narrow down, and to maintain the original angle of the edge bevel.

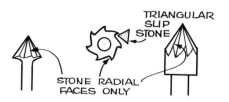

Fig. 6. Sharpen countersinks by stoning radial faces only.

COUNTERSINKS. You can sharpen these by handstoning the flat radial faces (the ones that lie on a radius). A triangular hard Arkansas slip is good for this. Don't use a soft stone; if it becomes grooved in use, it will envelop the sharp edges and soon dull them. Take care to keep the stone flat against the faces you are whetting; any tilt away from them will affect the edges. Figure 6 shows the whetting position. Don't try to whet the edges directly. This is almost sure to dull them, besides making some lower than the others, so that they no longer cut. Full reconditioning of multitoothed tools calls for a machine setup with provision for indexing.

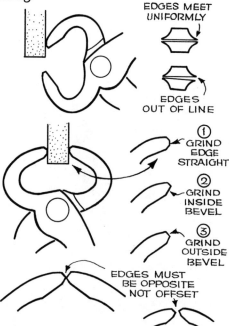

Fig. 7. Sharpening guide for carpenter's nippers, which should be ground in three stages.

CARPENTER'S NIPPERS. If the edges of these are beveled on the outside only, they can be sharpened on the side of a grinding wheel. Take care, though, to grind both edges exactly parallel to the pivot pin, so that they will meet along their full length, as shown in Figure 7.

Nipper edges that have both an inside and an outside bevel should be sharpened in three stages. First close the jaws gently on opposite sides of a thin wheel to dress down nicks and grind the jaws parallel. Next, grind a rather long bevel on the inside of each jaw. Take care that the bevels are of equal length and parallel to the pivot pin. Finally, grind the outer bevel so that the two edges meet squarely along their entire length.

SIDE-CUTTING PLIERS. A slipstone small enough to work between the opened jaws may be used to whet the edge bevels at their original angle. Some inexpensive pliers of this kind can even be filed (but don't expect that kind to stand up to much nail or wire clipping). A very small cone or cylindrical stone mounted in a high-speed hand grinder can also be used.

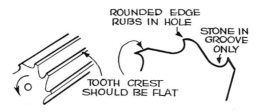

Fig. 8. Reamers should be sharpened by whetting the leading faces only. Do not stone the tops of the teeth, as this will change the tool's diameter.

REAMERS work much like countersinks, with the additional stress of being confined inside a hole. This greatly increases friction as soon as they become dull. Once the tooth crests are rounded by wear, they can only rub around inside, and the ensuing heat wears them even more quickly. Check the tooth crests with a good magnifying glass. At the first sign of rounding (Figure 8), whet the leading faces with a hard Arkansas stone. Don't use a soft stone.

The tops of the teeth should never be stoned, for this would change the working diameter of the reamer (which is usually a critical function of this tool). The faces, on the other hand, may be whetted several times without significant change in diameter.

Should the tooth crests be nicked or deeply rounded, the only way to salvage the tool is to grind all the teeth to a new and smaller diameter. This requires an indexed grinding setup.

TAPS AND DIES are usually the last things we suspect of being dull. Any extra effort in threading stock is blamed on the work material, its size, or that of the tapping hole. But the cutting edges of taps and dies do break down and become dull.

In principle, taps work much like reamer teeth; the leading edges do the cutting. The outer surfaces should not be touched, but taps can be sharpened by whetting that part of the grooves of flutes adjacent to the leading edges. Note (Figure 9) that this part is on the counterclockwise side of the edge as seen from the *bottom* end of the tap.

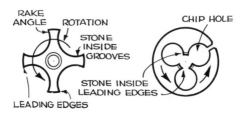

Fig. 9. Sharpen taps (left) by whetting the grooves adjacent to the leading edges. Dies can be sharpened (right) by whetting the sides of the chip holes adjacent to the leading edges.

You can whet these areas with a hard round slipstone or with a hard round-edged slip. Take care to control the whetting angle so as not to round off the cutting edges. Don't flatten or dub off the hook (rake angle) just under the teeth; it is essential to free cutting.

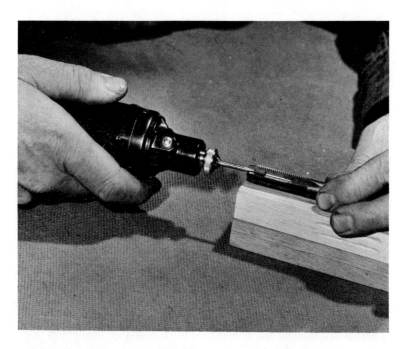

An electric hand grinder fitted with a small cylindrical stone can be used to sharpen taps if you work carefully. Grind in the groove along the leading edge of the teeth—the edge that bites in as the tap is turned.

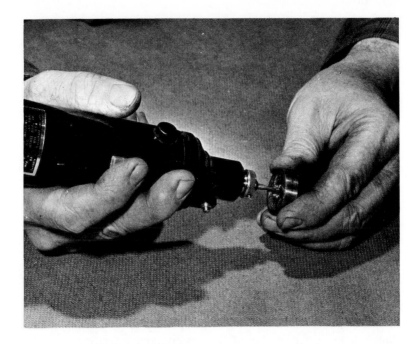

To sharpen dies, grind in the clearance holes. Be careful to retain the hook or rake angle between hole and leading edge. Rinse away grinding dust; it dulls the tool.

On dies, use a small, hard, round slipstone to whet the sides of the chip holes nearest the leading edges. Figure 9 shows these as seen from the underside of the die, the leading edges being on the left side of each chip hole. Seen from the top, they would be on the right side.

A small mounted stone in a hand grinder can be used to sharpen taps and dies, but good control is necessary not to let it climb (and dub off) the cutting edges. Use a magnifying glass to check the action of whetting or grinding.

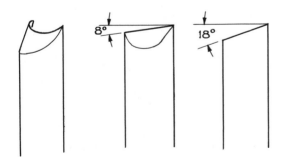

Fig. 10. Single-flute router bits have a single flat, but this must be whetted at the compound angle shown.

ROUTER BITS are chiefly of two types—single and double flute. Single-flute bits (Figure 10) are easier to sharpen, as it is only necessary to whet a single flat at the proper compound angle.

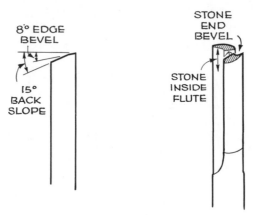

Fig. 11. Sharpening guide for double-flute router bits.

This flat has a back slope, but it also slants to the left. This gives it a clearance angle like that of a twist-drill lip, and for the same reason. The flat itself is a single surface, both back slope and clearance angles being formed simultaneously if it is held at the correct angle. You can whet it on a fine-grained wheel, with a hand slip, or on a bench stone. If whetting or grinding is done with the abrasive advancing against the edge (which is inside the single flute) no deburring is necessary.

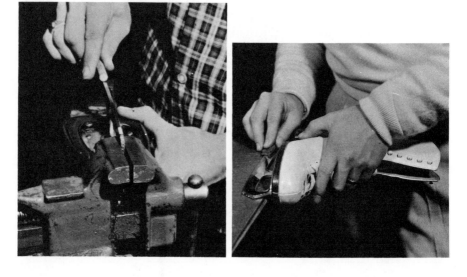

To sharpen ice skates, clamp the blade in a vise and hone the concave face of the blade with a fine India round file (left). Use oil to lubricate the stone and rotate it at each stroke to equalize the wear. Then lay the blade flat on the bench edge (right) and whet the side of the blade a few times with a flat India stone.

Double-flute router bits (Figure 11) have a fairly flat angle just behind each cutting edge, with a somewhat steeper angle behind that first one. Handstone one edge at a time, being careful not to cross over against the other (which slopes oppositely). Use a hard square or triangular abrasive file held at 8 degrees (or to the original bevel angle, if different on the bit in question). Some such bits have a single bevel only, which should be maintained in sharpening.

If the bit is damaged so that the edges must be reshaped, first grind the entire end across square. A good way to do this is to chuck the bit and lower it, while spinning, against a flat stone. Then grind the steeper back slopes, but stop so as to leave a narrow land behind each edge. Finally, whet these lands separately at 8 degrees, using a magnifying glass to watch the bevel as it grows wider. Stop as soon as it reaches the edge. If the end of the bit has been squared up as suggested above, the two edges should now be of exactly the same length, and the bit is ready for use.

ICE SKATES. Proper regrinding of skates requires a special grinding setup, with a fixture in which the skate can be clamped and traversed across the wheel face. It wouldn't pay the individual skater to invest in such, but he can touch up his skate blades between grinding intervals by handstoning.

Clamp the skate firmly in a vise, blade up. With a fine India round file held parallel to the blade, hone the concave face of the blade as shown in a photo. Using oil, rub the stone the full length of the blade several times, rotating it at each stroke to equalize wear on it and retain its shape. Wipe the blade dry and inspect it to see whether further honing is necessary.

Next, lay the blade with its edge flat on the edge of the bench, as shown in another photo. Rub a fine flat India stone flat against the side of the blade a few times as shown. Turn the skate over to hone the other edge the same way. Wipe off all oil and honing dust carefully before setting the skates aside.

CHAPTER NINE

TOOL BITS FOR THE
METAL-TURNING LATHE

THERE's nothing difficult about grinding good lathe bits if you remember a few facts about metals and bit angles. You can, in fact, grind better lathe bits than any you can expect to buy. Furthermore, you can grind special bits, for individual turning jobs, which you couldn't buy at all.

The business edge of a lathe bit, in order to stand up to the shock of parting off metal, must be much more obtuse than that of a knife or a woodworking tool. The bit must get under the surface of the metal, lift a chip, and carry it away continuously. Small wonder that the precise shape of a lathe bit is important. It must be ground to suit the work in hand, the kind of metal being turned, and the holder in which it is mounted.

READY-GROUND LATHE BITS. Being mass produced, these often show the grinding marks of the coarse-grit wheels used to shape them. These bits will do for rough turning, but you can improve their cutting action and the finish produced on the work by hand whetting them where it will count most.

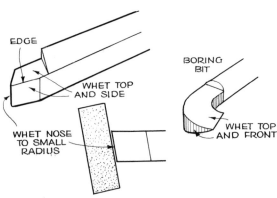

Fig. 1. Whetting ready-ground lathe bits.

This generally means the top and side surfaces which, where they meet, form the cutting edge (Figure 1). Hold a hard, fine-grit stone flat against each surface (or the bit against the stone) and whet until a narrow bright line appears along the edge. Provided it extends to the point, this is quite sufficient for the purpose—the whetting action need not show over the entire area. But holding the stone as if you were *trying* to whet the full surface is the easiest way to avoid rocking the bit or the stone and so rounding off the edge.

If the bit has a sharp point, round it off with a handstone to a very small radius; you'll get a better finish than from the point. But hold the stone against the entire front corner, not the point only, for this would change the front clearance angle. In the case of a boring bit, whet the front as well as the left side and the top.

A well-whetted tool should cut better, work with less lathe effort, and last longer than one used just as it comes from the grinder.

GRIND TOP OF BIT ONLY

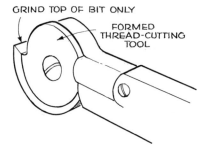

FORMED
THREAD-CUTTING
TOOL

Fig. 2. Grind only the top
of a formed threading bit.

SHARPENING USED BITS, if their only fault is that they have become dull, should be simply a matter of grinding the top and side surfaces at the original angles until the cutting edge is renewed. Take the time to set up the grinding rest accurately, or to align the bit against the wheel before you start it running, if doing the job freehand. Try to grind the entire surface in each case, not a corner here and an edge there. Then whet the side, top, and point for best results. But grind only the top of a threading bit of the kind in Figure 2, and only the front of a parting tool (Figure 3).

If your lathe bits have not been giving you good results, however, inspect them after looking at drawings that follow. You may have the wrong bits for your tool holder, or the wrong bit angles for the metal you wish to turn.

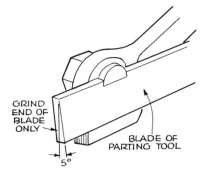

GRIND
END OF
BLADE
ONLY

BLADE OF
PARTING TOOL

5°

Fig. 3. Grind only the
front of a parting tool.

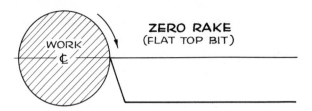

Fig. 4. Side view of tool bit with zero rake.

GRINDING YOUR OWN BITS. Many a time a lathe operator will want to grind a new tool. To do so, it's important to know some basic facts about tool angles. Figure 4 shows a typical tool bit as seen from its side. The edge presented to the revolving work is formed by the top and front surfaces. Because the top is parallel to the horizontal center line of the workpiece, this bit has zero rake angle, which is satisfactory for brass or bronze.

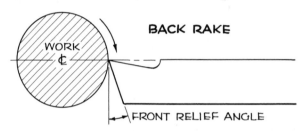

Fig. 5. Side view of tool bit with back rake.

Figure 5 shows a similar tool that has been ground to an angle behind the edge. Its top surface therefore presents a rake angle to the work. This back rake is desirable for steel, aluminum, some plastics, and some alloys.

In both cases the front of the bit is ground back at an angle to give the edge free access to the work without interference. This is the front relief or front clearance angle.

However, a tool for turning stock to a smaller diameter must be fed par-

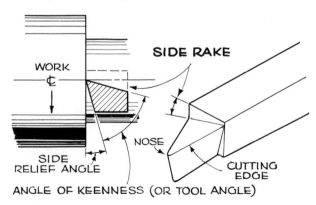

Fig. 6. Tool bit with side rake.

allel to the work axis and must do most of its cutting with a side edge, not one on the front only. Figure 6 shows a tool bit ground for this purpose. In addition to back rake as shown in Figure 5, it has been given side rake—that is, the top surface is ground at an angle in two directions, the leading corner and cutting edge being the highest parts. This tool has also been ground almost to a point, for a wide cutting edge works slowly, puts a heavy load on the lathe, and tends to chatter.

Furthermore, the left-hand side has been ground back under the cutting edge so that the edge is in advance of any other part and therefore free to cut into the work shoulder. Without this side-relief or side-clearance angle, the side of the tool would drag on the work and prevent entrance of the edge.

The angle between the side and the top surfaces is the angle of keenness. Something in the molecular structure of metals makes the best angle of keenness different for various materials. An angle of 60 degrees, for example, is efficient for turning soft steel. One of 70 degrees is good for ordinary cast iron, whereas for chilled iron it may be as great as 85 degrees.

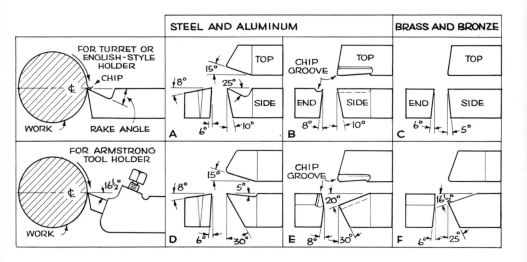

Fig. 7. Grinding lathe bits to suit holder and material.

The difference a holder makes. Standard tool bits are lengths of square-section steel, which must be clamped in a holder of some kind to do their work in the lathe. Open-side and turret tool posts hold the bit in a horizontal position as in Figures 4 and 5. But a popular tool holder that is standard equipment on many lathes (Figure 7) holds the bit shank at an angle of 16½ degrees to the horizontal.

Obviously this makes a big difference in the rake angle the bit presents to the work. The tool in Figure 4, if put into this holder, would have a positive rake angle of 16½ degrees instead of zero rake, while the bit in Figure 5 would have that much *more* back rake. In both cases, the front clearance angle would be greatly diminished, perhaps enough to cause rubbing below the edge. Therefore tool bits must be ground to suit the holder in which they are to be used.

One advantage of this type of holder (sometimes called the Armstrong holder) is that a steep rake angle may be achieved without grinding away so much of the tool bit as to weaken it. The bit at A in Figure 7 shows the difference in a typical bit ground for turning steel or aluminum. But for zero rake, the top of the bit must be ground down toward the edge by 16½ degrees to compensate for the Armstrong holder's upslant, like the tool at C in Figure 7.

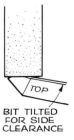

BIT TILTED
FOR SIDE
CLEARANCE

Fig. 8. Grinding the side of cutter bit.

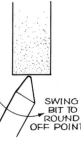

SWING
BIT TO
ROUND
OFF POINT

Fig. 9. Rounding the point of a cutter bit.

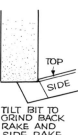

TILT BIT TO
GRIND BACK
RAKE AND
SIDE RAKE

Fig. 10. Grinding side and back rake of cutter bit.

Grinding cutter bits. For shaping (rather than sharpening), a 36-grit wheel should be available. Finish grinding may then be done on a finer wheel to minimize grinding marks before whetting.

Bit blanks have beveled ends, which reduce the amount of grinding necessary to form the front clearance angle. Any grinding required may be done on the face of the wheel. The sides are ground as in Figure 8, the tool rest being tilted (or the bit held at an angle) to form the side clearance. The point may be rounded by swinging the bit against the wheel face as in Figure 9.

Side and back rake are ground on the top simultaneously by holding the bit against the wheel at an appropriate angle as in Figure 10. In all cases, try to grind a single continuous surface on the bit, not a series of facets or a curved surface. Take care to avoid overheating. A loaded wheel will remove stock slowly and overheat the bit. Dress the wheel, if necessary, to insure free grinding. Finish bits by hand honing, unless they are for roughing cuts only.

Typical tool bits for use in the Armstrong type of holder are shown in Figure 11. A roughing tool is for removing stock rapidly with moderately deep cuts (up to $\frac{1}{8}$" on a 9" lathe, for example). This is a right-hand tool, probably the most commonly used type. It is fed from right to left, toward the headstock. The less commonly used left-hand turning tool is for feeding from left to right, toward the tailstock.

The right-hand side tool is for facing work in the chuck, or for facing the right side of shoulders. It is ground to a 58-degree point so that the right side of the bit will just clear the tailstock center when facing a shoulder square. The point is sharp. Such a bit is best fed out from the center toward the operator. A left-hand side tool is for facing left-hand shoulders, but otherwise is identical to a right-hand side tool. These bits have right or left-hand side rake as the case may require.

The round-nose tool, on the other hand, has no side rake at all because it is meant to be fed either way—for turning both surfaces of a shoulder, or for necking down an intermediate part of a shaft, for example. Though ground parallel to the shank on top, it does have back rake when used in an Armstrong-type holder. Grind the top to slope *down* at 16½ degrees, however, and you have a useful zero-rake bit for turning brass or bronze.

The threading tool too, if ground for an Armstrong holder, must slope down so that it will have zero rake. The point should be sharp, and the bit must have ample side clearance on both sides.

To grind the other bits for an open-side or turret tool post, the back-rake angle must be increased 16½ degrees by grinding down into the bit, and the front clearance angle decreased accordingly, especially for heavy cuts. Side rake and side clearance angles remain the same. Except on side and threading tools, it's best to whet sharp points to a small radius.

A front clearance angle of 8 degrees (measured from a vertical tangent of the workpiece as in Figure 5, not on the bit itself) is adequate for most bits to be used on steel. Side rake may be from 12 to 22 degrees, the lower figure for such tough metals as chrome vanadium steel, the higher for easily machined steels. About 14 degrees of side rake is enough for all carbon steels and the more machinable nickel alloy steels.

Side clearance should be from 10 to 12 degrees. A back-rake angle of 16½ degrees (the cutting edge being parallel to the shank for use in an Armstrong holder) is good for most carbon steels. This back rake blends with the side rake, of course, the true rake angle being a combination of both. For nickel alloys the top should be ground to slope down to the front, so decreasing the back rake to 12 degrees, or for very tough materials to as little as 8 degrees.

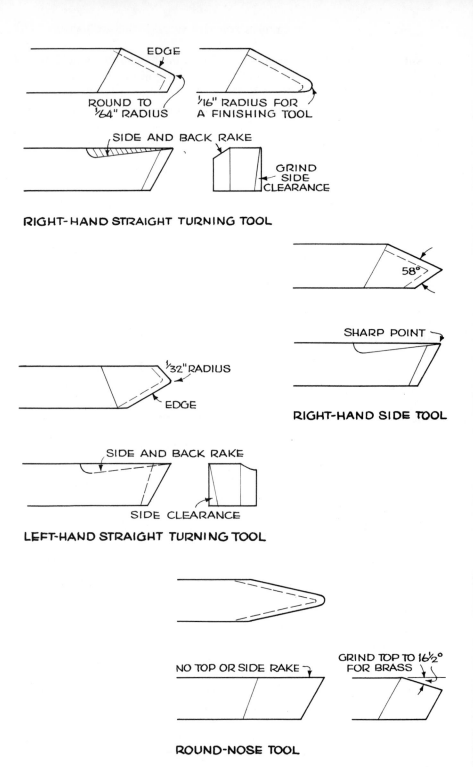

EDGE

ROUND TO 1/64" RADIUS

1/16" RADIUS FOR A FINISHING TOOL

SIDE AND BACK RAKE

GRIND SIDE CLEARANCE

RIGHT-HAND STRAIGHT TURNING TOOL

58°

SHARP POINT

1/32" RADIUS

EDGE

RIGHT-HAND SIDE TOOL

SIDE AND BACK RAKE

SIDE CLEARANCE

LEFT-HAND STRAIGHT TURNING TOOL

NO TOP OR SIDE RAKE

GRIND TOP TO 16½° FOR BRASS

ROUND-NOSE TOOL

Fig. 11. Tool bits for use in an Armstrong type of holder.

The magic chip groove. The bits so far described are standard and should give good service. But some experienced machinists grind a groove just behind the cutting edge of their bits as at B in Figure 7. This does several things. It replaces conventional side and back rake angles with a very steep side-rake angle—the slope of the groove itself. It curls up chips into tight little spirals that flow away from the work instead of tangling with it and the bit. Properly ground chip grooves leave a good finish, and take deep cuts with less effort than conventional tools. Chip-groove bits are chiefly for turning steel, aluminum, and certain plastics. They should never be used for brass, bronze, or cast iron.

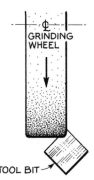

Fig. 12. Grinding a chip groove
in a tool bit.

Grinding a chip groove is easier than it looks. First grind the tip shape and clearance angles, leaving the top of the bit flat. Then put in the groove with a corner of the grinding wheel as in Figure 12, making the groove deepest at the end and letting it taper to shallowness toward the shank. (On some tools shown farther on, the groove may be of uniform width.) To be effective, the groove must extend to the very edge. Whet the edge as usual after grinding.

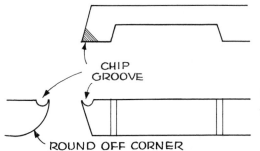

Fig. 13. Boring bit with a chip
groove ground across corner.

With such a groove back of it, the edge is laterally weak and may break if the bit is rammed carelessly into stationary work. But with due care it is durable and stays sharp surprisingly long.

A chip groove can be ground on almost any shape of bit. The one in Figure 7 is capable of taking deep turning or facing cuts in steel even on light lathes, with no chatter, and leaves a nice finish. On aluminum it will take even deeper cuts at higher speeds.

A small boring bit made from a standard blank is shown in Figure 13. For steel or aluminum, carefully grind a small chip groove across the corner. Hone the front and side surfaces afterwards.

For use on steel, aluminum, and plastics, even a threading tool can be improved with a chip groove. Grind the sharp 60-degree tip with a flat top as usual. Then grind a groove parallel to the left-hand side as in Figure 14. Set the compound rest at 29 degrees for thread cutting, and advance the bit into the work between passes with the compound feed only.

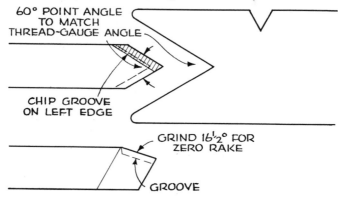

60° POINT ANGLE
TO MATCH
THREAD-GAUGE ANGLE

CHIP GROOVE
ON LEFT EDGE

GRIND 16½° FOR
ZERO RAKE

GROOVE

Fig. 14. Threading tool with chip groove.

A double-edged bit with two chip grooves can do three operations as shown in Figure 15. Fed straight in, its near corner (at the bottom in the drawing) bores the hole to size. Fed against the end of the bore, the left-hand edge chamfers the inner diameter. Moved outwards and fed against the rim, the right-hand edge of the bit chamfers the outer work diameter.

An unusual boring bar that brings two bores to diameter at once is shown in Figure 16. The part just behind each cutting corner is ground back slightly for clearance in the bore, and a tiny chip groove is ground diagonally across each of the cutting edges.

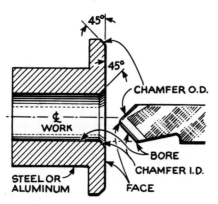

45°

45°

CHAMFER O.D.

₵
WORK

BORE

CHAMFER I.D.

STEEL OR
ALUMINUM

FACE

Fig. 15. Double-edged bit with two chip grooves can do three operations.

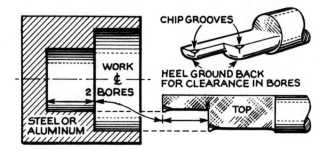

Fig. 16. Boring bar brings two bores to diameter at once.

Lathe bits of drill rod. For brass and soft steel, you can grind or even file bits from ¼″ drill rod. After cutting 1″ lengths, make a flat along each piece (Figure 17). This will orient the bit in the tool holder. Then grind the front and sides as shown. Finally, heat red hot and quench in water or oil.

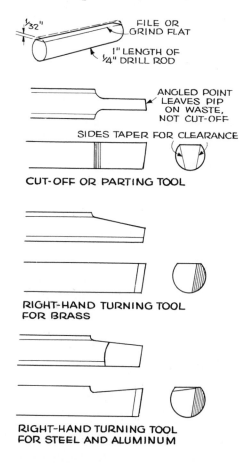

Fig. 17. Lathe bits of drill rod for brass and soft steel.

So hardened, the bits will stand up to turning soft steel, and they may be ground with back and side rake or even chip grooves if desired. Though they can't be expected to stand up to heavy work like high-speed steel bits, they are useful for delicate turning and to supplement the standard bits supplied with small lathes. The drill-rod bits can be clamped directly into the open-side tool holders furnished with some light lathes. For use in standard tool-posts, make a holder of ⅜″ by 1″ cold-rolled steel as in Figure 18. Drill the socket at a height that will put the *flats* of the bits exactly at lathe center height.

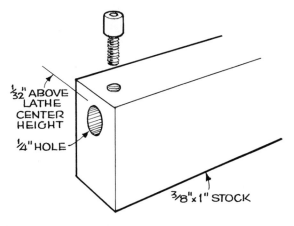

Fig. 18. Holder for use in standard tool-posts.

MAKE CENTER HEIGHT A HABIT. Set all bit points at exactly lathe center height. Even the best tool won't work if it is improperly set up. Setting a bit too high, for example, may negate the front clearance and make the front rub, while lifting the edge out of contact with the work. Set below center height, the edge scrapes the work at a negative rake angle. It can't cut well, any more than you can whittle with a knife slanted away from the direction of cut.

Though some machinists (and instruction manuals) advocate setting bits slightly above center for turning steel, the beginner will do better to stick to center-height setting in all cases. As fringe benefits, he will find it easier to standardize his tool grinding, and the cross-feed graduations on the lathe will mean exactly what they say. If the bit is high or low, they don't indicate tool advance with 100-percent accuracy.

A photo shows how a light rule may be used to tell whether the bit point is at center height. One lathe maker suggests scribing a line at that height on the end of the tailstock ram. By running the carriage over, any tool may quickly be set to the mark.

TOOL CHATTER is a vibration that leaves a rough finish on the work and is hard on the lathe and operator. Chatter is very likely to occur whenever the cutting edge of the bit in contact with the work is too wide. Parting-off and

To check whether bit is at center height, gently pinch a light rule between its tip and chucked piece of round stock. If the top tilts away, the tool is high; if toward you, it's low; if vertical as above, the bit is at the correct lathe center height.

grooving tools are persistent offenders in this respect. The blade of such tools must be at exactly 90 degrees to the work axis, and their points exactly at center height.

However, chatter is not always the fault of the tool. It may be due to loose spindle bearings, play in the crossfeed screw, loose gibs on the carriage, cross feed or compound feed, or a bit that projects too far from its holder. Digging or "hogging in" may result from the same faults, or from improper tool angles or tool adjustment. Zero-rake tools like parting-off and thread cutting bits, when used on steel, should be kept flooded with a cutting lubricant.

For heavy cuts especially, the tool holder should be clamped at 90 degrees to the work axis or even slanted slightly toward the tailstock. Cutting stresses will then tend to swing the bit out, or away from the work. If the holder is angled even slightly toward the headstock, a heavy cut that tends to swing the holder to the right will force the bit more deeply into the work. The probable result is a rough surface, tearing, or other damage to the work or th tool bit.

CHAPTER TEN

THE STUFF TOOLS ARE MADE OF

INEXTRICABLY linked with man's development of tools is the story of metals. Smelting was undoubtedly an accidental discovery, made before the dawn of recorded history. It was then found that certain earths, when highly heated, left a residue that solidified on cooling to something different from stone, which could be hammered, shaped, and sharpened to an edge.

The chemistry involved, though not understood until recent times, is simple. Metallic ores are generally oxides—compounds in which the metal is combined with oxygen. If heated with coke or charcoal, which like most fuels gives off carbon monoxide (a gas that greedily seeks another oxygen atom) the ore will lose its oxygen to the monoxide, a process called "reduction" by chemists. Thus, the ore is converted to metal plus slag and certain other impurities.

THE BRONZE AGE. Copper can be smelted from its óres at a lower temperature than iron, and largely for that reason came into wide use first. Pure copper is too soft for most practical purposes of weaponry or tool making, but it was discovered that the addition of tin would harden it. The proportion of tin used would, in fact, give it various characteristics. By 2,000 B.C. men knew how to make different types of the copper-tin alloy called bronze, some for weapons, others for metallic mirrors, shields, bells, and tableware.

Brass is chiefly an alloy of copper and zinc instead of tin. There are today quite a number of different brass compositions. Some contain aluminum, iron and tin in addition to zinc. But as edge-sustaining metals, bronze and brass soon gave way before iron and steel, once man learned to smelt ferric ores.

THE COMING OF IRON. Aside from fragments of meteoric iron, which they did not identify as such, early smiths sometimes found pellets of iron in the slag remaining from smelting other metal. It was eventually discovered that these iron nuggets could be heated and then hammered together to make larger pieces. Such wrought iron wasn't at first superior to bronze—it was in fact not as hard.

But about 1,400 B.C. certain Greek smiths found that reheating it repeatedly in a charcoal fire, and hammering it, would transform iron into something much harder than bronze. This was probably the first instance of case-hardening; the iron absorbed extra carbon from the fuel and so developed a hard shell of carbon-iron alloy, or steel, around a softer core.

Elsewhere it was discovered that plunging the red-hot metal into cold water would render it extremely hard, although often so brittle that it broke when subjected to shock. The solution to this, found in the Roman era, was to reheat it gently and quench it again at a much lower heat. So treated, the metal retained much of its hardness while losing its extreme brittleness. A steel dagger was found in the tomb of Tutankhamon (1,350 B.C.) and the Hittites of Biblical time were iron and steel makers.

THE ROLE OF CARBON. Carbon is an element most commonly encountered in the form of electric-motor and generator brushes, or the center elements in dry cells. A French chemist in 1722 was first to make it clear that the proportion of carbon in iron was the key to steel making. But iron itself may be of very low or very high carbon content. Open-hearth iron has almost no carbon (perhaps .025 percent) whereas pig iron and cast iron usually have over 3.00 percent.

Cast iron and wrought iron were still used for bridges, rails, and railroad rolling stock well into the 19th century, although the superiority of steel was abundantly evident (a steel rail was said to outlast an iron rail 20 to one). Sir Henry Bessemer's invention of the converter in 1856, followed by William Kelly's parallel invention in America in 1862, marked the beginning of big steel production.

Converters blow an air blast into molten pig iron. The oxygen in the air blast combines with silicon, manganese, and carbon in the iron, so refining it. After the "blow" is over, controlled quantities of carbon or other alloying elements are added to make the kind of steel desired. Alloy steels, which may contain small amounts of tungsten, chromium, nickel, manganese and vanadium, came gradually into use for special purposes, tool making among them. Today there are three other methods of steelmaking—the crucible, open-hearth, and electric processes.

MATERIALS FOR TOOL MAKING. In a narrow range of carbon content there are low, medium, and high-carbon steels for many important purposes. Sheet steel used for drawing and stamping has as little as .04 percent carbon, low-carbon structural steel from .08 to .25 percent. Intermediate-carbon steels for rails, springs, railroad-car axles, and some shock-resisting tools contain from .45 to .75 percent carbon.

In steel for drills, reamers, ball bearings, and drill rod, the carbon content may be from .75 to 1.25 percent. In the form of drill rod, this *high-carbon steel* can be purchased in many well-stocked hardware stores as well as from machinery and mill supply dealers. Tool steel, used for dies, files, and other tools requiring great abrasion resistance, has still a higher percentage of carbon. Tools of such carbon steels can be made very hard, but if overheated by grinding, or by excessive work loads, their hardness is drawn or lost.

High-speed steel is a term applied to a number of alloys containing tungsten, molybdenum, vanadium, nickel, or manganese. These have some startling properties quite unlike those of carbon steels. The foremost one is that high-speed steel will stay hard at temperatures that instantly soften hardened tool steels. With high-speed-steel tools, machining may be done at speeds that heat the chips to a dull red. This is the reason for the "high speed" designation.

However, heat treatment does not make these steels quite as hard as it can tool or carbon steel. High-speed steel is also much more difficult to harden, its absorption point (the temperature at which it turns hard) being in the white-hot range. Brought to this heat, it will then harden on cooling in air, without quenching. For this reason such steels are sometimes termed "air hardening" or "self hardening."

Since they do cool hard in air, they are difficult to anneal or soften. For this they must be packed in an airtight case, the case and all being heated white hot and cooled down very gradually. Tempering is also in a different heat range than for carbon steel—from blue to dull cherry red. Tempering greatly increases the toughness of high-speed steel.

Stainless steels appeared about 1913, when it was found that adding chromium made steel rust resistant, and that the addition of nickel further changed its characteristics. Some chromium steels are hardenable, and used for making cutlery. Others are not hardenable by heat treatment, but change their characteristics when cold-worked by drawing, rolling, or spinning.

Tungsten carbide is a common term for two tungsten alloys trade-named Carboloy and Stellite. These have little iron in them; Stellite, for example, is composed chiefly of chromium, cobalt, carbon, and tungsten, with only traces of iron, silicon, and manganese. Being almost diamond hard, these tungsten alloys cannot be machined, but only ground. Tools are usually made of a steel body or shank, to which pieces of tungsten carbide are cemented.

Such tools can machine metal at three times the speed of high-speed steel, and can work at red heat. The corrosion resistance of tungsten carbide also adapts it to such special applications as surgical instruments and optical mirrors. Nowadays it's even found on the newer electric carving knives.

SPARKS IDENTIFY THE METAL. It is often important to know whether you're working with wrought iron, cast iron, or cold-rolled steel, or whether a tool is of carbon or high-speed steel. The kind of sparks the metal produces when ground can give some useful clues, for although at first all grinding sparks may seem alike, they are in fact quite different for different metals.

Those with iron and oxygen in their composition commonly generate brilliant sparks. Spurts, stars, or bursts occur only when carbon is present. Nonferrous metals like brass, aluminum, copper, and bronze produce no sparks.

Figure 1 shows the color and types of sparks to be expected from six ferrous metals. The spark stream from some changes color at a distance from the wheel. The descriptions are, of course, relative. Spark length and abun-

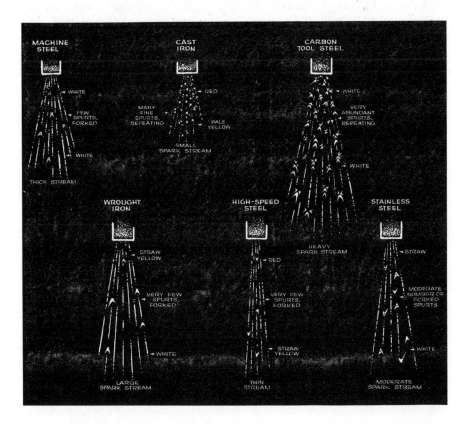

Fig. 1. Reading spark signals to identify metals. The actual length and thickness of the spark streams will depend on grinding pressure, the hardness and condition of the wheel, and the metal itself. Grind at a point on the wheel that will allow the sparks to fly off for some distance, so that you can compare their color near the wheel with that at the end of the stream. "Forked" spurts mean those that seem to branch off only once from a single spark. "Repeating" spurts appear to branch and rebranch. Sparks from *manganese* steel are very like those from *carbon* steel, and of similar volume, so these two metals are hard to tell apart. Some cast iron produces a smaller spark stream than that shown, with fewer spurts. Tungsten carbide creates a very small spark stream, orange to light orange in color, with no spurts. If possible, grind known samples to learn spark identification.

dance, for instance, depends in part on grinding pressure; color may be affected by the light in which you view it. Shadowed daylight is perhaps best; turn off nearby lights to let the sparks show better.

The grinding wheel used isn't critical, though it should be in good shape so as to grind freely. Use light pressure to avoid wasting metal and to keep the spark stream steady long enough to evaluate it. If possible, get some known samples of the various metals, grind them, and add your own notations to the chart.

HEAT-TREATING CARBON STEEL calls for comparatively simple equipment, unless intricate shapes or large quantities are handled. For small tools, you can manage with a propane torch, a couple of fire brick or asbestos blocks, and tongs. Bricks or blocks can be arranged to form an enclosure that will confine and reflect the heat of the torch. Some small pieces might even be hardened and tempered by the use of an electric hot plate with an oven-glass (Pyrex) dish as a hood. But for large pieces you'll need a furnace or a smith's fire.

If you're rehardening a tool that has been hardened before, or want to soften a hard workpiece so that it can be filed or machined, the first step is annealing. This means bringing the piece to a good red heat all over, and letting it cool as slowly as possible. The best way to do this is in a furnace, letting it and the work cool off slowly together. Lacking a furnace, you can heat the piece with a torch, preferably shielded from drafts with asbestos blocks (or rolled into asbestos paper) and withdraw or turn down the flame slowly after the piece is red hot throughout. (Exact-size tools like reamers should be shut in an air-tight box, and the box heated to full redness and allowed to cool before opening.)

Annealing is a good idea even if you're making a new tool from a piece of carbon steel. It relieves internal stresses left by rolling or other manufacturing processes.

To harden carbon steel, bring it up to red heat slowly, especially in the first or black-hot stage. Once it begins to glow, heating may be more rapid. Apply heat at the thickest section; it will travel to thinner ones, which are more readily overheated. Turn the piece around often, if heating it from one side. Hold heat back from thin edges or points; if made white hot, these may be "burned" and the piece will be ruined. You don't have to heat the entire piece, however, if hardness is required only at one end. But do try to avoid a sharp cut-off line between the black-hot and red-hot portions.

The right hardening heat is a bright cherry red as seen in daytime shadow. It can even be bright red, but at yellow-red heat the piece may crack when quenched, or become excessively brittle.

Grasp the hot piece with tongs away from the glowing section (which the tongs will otherwise cool prematurely). Plunge it in cold water, preferably end first, and stir it about. If you leave it motionless in the water, the steam jacket that forms around the red-hot metal will keep the water away and prevent swift quenching. Leave the piece in the water until it is cool enough to handle.

Adding salt to the water will make it quench steel so quickly as to crack it, while soap will slow quenching to make the steel less hard or even leave it soft. Small quantities of either may be added to the quenching water when desirable. Thin oil is also a less drastic quenching medium.

Test the hardened section with a file. Don't actually file it, but just try to get a "bite" on it. If the file teeth simply skate over the metal, the steel is "dead hard." If they bite, it's not. Experts can tell dead-hard steel by its appearance, but the simple file test is surer for most of us. If the steel is dark blue after quenching, however, it's fairly certain that it either wasn't hot enough for hardening, or is a type with insufficient carbon for hardening in this way.

TEMPERING IS THE KEY to good tools. In the dead-hard state, steel is too brittle to stand up under the shock of cutting, chopping, or machining. A second heat treatment—tempering—is vital.

This is entirely different from annealing. It is a carefully limited, partial softening only. It takes place at much lower temperatures than annealing does, and within a very narrow range—from 430 to 600 degrees Fahrenheit. By reheating a dead-hard piece of steel somewhere within that range, and again quenching it to "fix" its condition, you can leave it in a state of hardness best suited to its purpose.

A machinist's scraper might be tempered at the lowest heat (430 degrees), which will still leave it quite hard. A cold chisel or an auger bit, on the other hand, will be reheated to a higher temperature. Though rendered softer by this, and therefore needing more frequent sharpening, the tool is less brittle and better able to withstand its working stress.

Fortunately you don't need a thermometer to gauge tempering temperatures. If dead-hard steel is brightened with steel wool or abrasive paper, or by light filing or grinding, heating it will give it a coating of oxide. This film gradually thickens as the temperature of the piece goes up, and it changes color as it does so.

The oxide colors are an almost infallible guide to the temperature of the metal at any point. They change as follows: First to appear on the bright surface is a pale yellow tinge corresponding to 430 degrees F. A little more heat changes it to a yellow faintly tinged with red and a little darker, or a pale straw color (450 degrees). A still deeper or middle straw color is 475 degrees, while dark red-brown is 500 degrees. Further heating darkens this to purple, indicating 535 degrees, and still more heat makes the red die out, leaving deep blue, which is 570 degrees. Above that the blue becomes brighter, then green-tinged (about 600) and green-grey.

These colors travel progressively along the workpiece from the area to which heat is applied, so by watching them you can leave any part as hard or soft as you wish. Having made a tool, for example, dead hard, grind the cutting edge or edges and brighten the metal for some distance back. Don't apply a flame directly to the edges, but some distance away—to the shank or even at the other end. Use a small flame, turning the tool to keep the heat uniform all around. Always point the flame away from the edge; heat extends well past the visible part of the flame, and if it is aimed at a point or an edge, it may anneal this long before you are aware that it's happening.

Having adequate light to judge the tempering colors by, watch them creep from the heated portion toward the edge. As soon as the desired color (and tempering heat) reaches the edge, immediately quench the piece in cold water.

Experienced workers sometimes use the blacksmith's one-heat method of hardening and tempering, doing them almost simultaneously. The piece is made a little hotter than necessary for hardening, and over more of its length. The end to be hardened is then quenched in water for a short distance from the edge or point by dipping it up and down for say ¾" to avoid a sharp border line between hard and soft sections.

With the end cold, the tool is laid on a brick or asbestos block and the hard part quickly brightened with abrasive paper or a bit of stone. One has to work fast, for heat is already being conducted to that end from the still-hot shank. Tempering colors will swiftly appear on the cleaned portion, and as soon as the right one reaches the edge, the entire tool should be quenched.

Instead of a torch, a thick piece of steel or iron (the sole plate of an old electric iron, for example) may be heated red hot in a fire and used for tempering. Hold small workpieces above the red-hot surface, not touching it. A metal plate on an electric stove may also be used. Tools that come to a point or a thin edge may be held with the thick end nearest the hot surface. The conduction of tempering heat may be slowed by holding thinner parts with tongs, which will dissipate some of the heat and so give better control.

CASEHARDENING is a process of developing a hard steel shell on the outside of softer steel, wrought iron, or even cast iron. This is a good way to surface-harden steel of a composition that cannot be hardened by heating and quenching. It is also valuable for machine parts like gears, the teeth of which must stand up to severe surface wear but must not be so brittle as to shatter under driving shocks. However, a casehardened shell may be too thin for tools that must be resharpened by grinding.

Charred bone and leather were among the first casehardening agents, followed by such poisonous chemicals as potassium cyanide. Now there are casehardening compounds that do a good job with none of the health hazards cyanide involves. With these, iron and mild steel can be made hard enough to stand up to work otherwise quite beyond such metals. You can, for example, make a punch from an ordinary nail.

To harden mild-steel parts with such a compound, first heat the piece as evenly as possible to a bright red. Immediately dip or roll it in the com-

HOW TO USE TEMPERING COLORS

COLOR	TEMPERATURE	SUITABLE FOR
Very pale yellow	430°	Scrapers, gravers, hand turning tools
Pale straw (yellow)	450°	End mills, milling cutters, lathe bits, boring bits
Middle straw	475°	Taps and dies, thread chasers, knurling wheels, wood bits, counterbores, countersinks
Dark straw (red-brown)	500°	Twist drills, flat drills for iron, plane irons, chisels, gouges
Purple	535°	Center punches, lathe centers, leather punches, flat drills for brass, scissors, table knives
Blue	570°	Cold chisels, auger bits, circular saws, saws for metal
Blue-green	600°	Screwdrivers, springs, saws for wood

pound, which should form a melted coating on the metal. Then reheat the piece again to bright red, and quench it in cold water.

The depth of the case may be increased by repeating the treatment one or more times, or by packing the workpiece in a container (such as a piece of pipe) with hardening compound around it, and heating everything cherry red for up to half an hour before quenching.

Cast iron and tool steel can also be casehardened. Follow the special instructions provided; it may be necessary to heat these metals more than mild steel.

SIMPLE TOOLS YOU CAN MAKE. Old files, first annealed and then rehardened and tempered, can be used to make scrapers, gravers, turning chisels, form tools, and others. If little reshaping is required, and the tool's purpose involves no stress likely to snap the rather brittle file metal, annealing is not necessary. The working part can be shaped by grinding.

A useful three-edged scraper can be made by hollow-grinding the three surfaces of a good-sized triangular file as in Figure 2. The safest if not the most accurate way to do this is probably freehand. Should you use the grinding rest, set it close to and low on the wheel. Take great care not to let the corner of the file wedge between rest and wheel, nor allow the top corner to tilt up and dig into the wheel. Hold the file firmly down on the rest, but only lightly against the wheel.

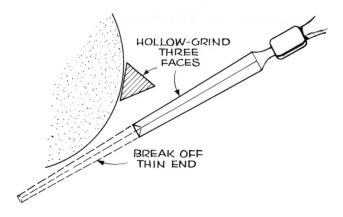

Fig. 2. Scraper made by hollow grinding triangular file.

Small gouges for carving and model work can be made of umbrella ribs and fitted with suitable handles. For light occasional work they may be used unhardened, though you might want to try both ordinary hot quenching and casehardening of the umbrella ribs.

Small reamers that will bring a hole close to their own exact size can be made of drill rod or other round stock as shown in Figure 3. Drill rod is ground to a good finish and to standard sizes, though it may vary a thousandth or two from piece to piece. Check it with a micrometer if size is critical. However, if the shaft or other piece required to fit the hole is made of the same stock as the reamer, the hole will be just the right size.

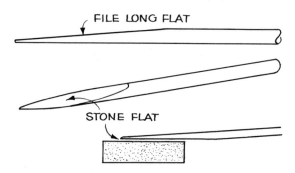

Fig. 3. Reamer made from drill rod or other round stock.

To make this kind of reamer, simply file or grind a long, tapering flat on the stock. Be sure to keep the surface flat its full width, for the edge is formed where it meets the circumference of the stock. Take care not to overheat, bend, or warp the piece when forming the flat. Protect the polished rod surface by using soft jaws in the vise, or shielding it from those of pliers.

For use on brass, the reamer need not be hardened. Finish it by stoning the flat until all grinding or file marks are gone, leaving the edge sharp. In removing any burr or false edge, stone the round side only very lightly, for removing metal here will impair the reamer's cutting power.

A nonchattering countersink may be made of drill rod, turned in a lathe as in Figure 4. The straight flat is then filed, leaving slightly more than half the diameter intact. Like the reamer, this tool cuts along one of its edges only, the other steadying it in the hole. For sharpening, stone the flat face only—and sparingly, for when it is down to less than half the diameter, the tool will no longer work well. For all-around use, harden and temper the countersink, quenching it at middle-straw heat. You can make it cut more freely by stoning some clearance on the half-cone point behind the cutting edge, as in a twist drill, but too much clearance will make it likely to chatter.

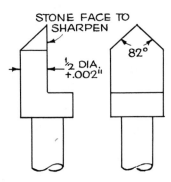

Fig. 4. Countersink made of drill rod.

D-bits are for enlarging a hole started by another drill, and are handy if you haven't the exact size available in a commercial drill. They should be used in a drill press or a lathe, where work and drill can be pre-aligned. D-bits cut along one axial edge and at the corner or point. To make them, grind or file away almost—but not quite—half the diameter as shown in Figure 5.

The D-shaped end is then given a back slope of about 5 degrees as shown, and an equal end bevel, after which the tool may be hardened and tempered to dark straw.

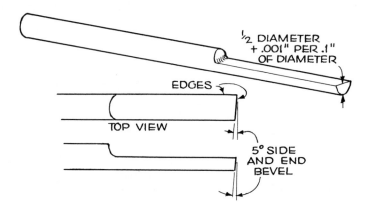

Fig. 5. D-bit for use in drill press or lathe.

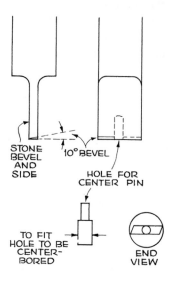

Fig. 6. Counterbore made of drill rod stock.

The counterbore in Figure 6 will form a flat-bottomed recess in a hole to receive a fillister-head or socket-head screw. This tool is easier to make if the drill-rod stock is first centerdrilled to take a removable center pin, rather than turning a solid pin on the stock. The removable pin makes it much easier to shape and sharpen the cutting edges, and pins may be interchanged to fit different pilot-hole sizes.

File flats on opposite sides of the center hole. Then bevel their tops in opposite directions. For free cutting, it's a good idea to form a small clearance angle on the outside as shown in the end view. Harden, temper, and stone the edges and front faces.

Flat drills of either standard or odd sizes, which will originate holes in wood or metal, can be made of drill rod (or of mild steel rod, if casehard-

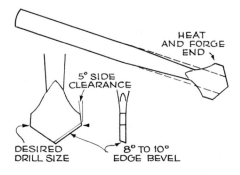

Fig. 7. Flat drill made of drill rod or casehardened mild steel rod.

ened). Heat the end red hot and hammer it flat as shown in Figure 7, taking care to keep the tip symmetrical and the flattened area central to the shank. File or grind the point accurately to shape and size.

The one-heat method may be used for hardening and tempering. Heat half the length from the point bright cherry red. Plunge an inch of the end into cold water, stirring gently. Quickly brighten one side of the end, watch the tempering colors appear, and requench the whole tool when the point is dark straw or, for use in brass, purple. Then grind the clearance on the edges and sides, and whet to keenness.

INDEX